RUSSIA UNDER
CATHERINE THE GREAT

RUSSIA UNDER
CATHERINE THE GREAT

VOLUME ONE:
SELECT DOCUMENTS ON
GOVERNMENT AND SOCIETY

Translated and introduced
by
Paul Dukes, Reader in History,
Aberdeen University

Oriental Research Partners
Newtonville
1978

ISBN (cloth) 0-89250-104-9
      (paper) 0-89250-105-7

This is volume I of *Russia under Catherine the Great*. Volume II, *Catherine the Great's Instruction (NAKAZ) to the Legislative Commission, 1767* was published in 1977.

Readers may obtain a catalogue of our publications by writing to the Editor,
Dr. P.H. Clendenning,
Oriental Research Partners,
Box 158, Newtonville, Mass. 02160.

Printed and bound in England by The Burlington Press

For Taffy and Joyce

CONTENTS

    a) Popular Satire
    b) The Edicts of Pugachev
    c) Governmental Manifestos on Pugachev
    d) Pugachev's Testimony at the Interrogation in Iaik Town, 16 September 1774
    e) A Contemporary Noble writes about Pugachev

Preface

This book originated as a labour of obligation rather than of love, when colleagues who had not yet broken the language barrier urged me to undertake a series of translations. The choice of documents was partly governed by their suggestions, which stemmed not only from an interest in Russian history but also a concern with its international context. For example, the decrees on the nobility were selected to some extent as a basis for the comparative consideration of European nobilities, Polenov's observations on serfdom for possible inclusion in the even wider setting of slavery and emancipation. Another good reason for the work and further determinant of its contents was the circumstance that nearly all history students at the University of Aberdeen did not have the language requirement for getting at Russian documents in the original. These two sets of motives have not seemed incompatible, and the results could be of interest to readers other than those prompting them.

Touching on matters from lofty philosophical abstraction, which occupied no more than a few, to the mundane business of the farming year, which would be the outward concern of the vast majority, I hope to have provided a composite if extremely impressionistic picture of government and society under Catherine the Great. The Table of Ranks was an integral part, even the keystone, of the imperial edifice constructed by Peter the Great and fundamentally unchanged at the accession of Catherine in 1762. Tatischev's *Dissertation* was probably the first mature modern piece of Russian political thought, concerning many of the questions that Catherine was to address in her *Instructions.* The Emancipation of the Nobility, a decree issued by her husband a few months before her accession, has often been considered to have changed significantly the relationship between the government and the ruling class. With the scene now set for her arrival, Catherine's directions to one of her most important early appointments, A.A. Viazemskii as Procurator-General, illustrate many aspects of her avowed intentions. Her larger and more theoretical statement in this direction, her *Instructions,* comprise the second volume of these documents, but included here in the first volume is S.E. Desnitskii's *Proposal,* which was submitted to the Empress as an aid to the completion of the great task for which she had summoned her Legislative Commission and

1

which also had a direct influence on one of the supplements to her *Instructions*. No problem confronted Catherine at this time as great as serfdom, and we turn next to consider a comprehensive answer by A. Ia. Polenov to a Prize Essay question essentially on this subject set by the Empress just before her summons of the Commission. The work of the serfs as viewed from above is the principal theme of the next document, an answer by P.I. Rychkov to another Prize Essay question, how to compose instructions for a steward or bailiff. We then look at some attitudes to work and other problems from below, in three examples of popular satire composed in the decades leading up to the greatest outbreak of domestic violence in Catherine's reign, the Pugachev Revolt of 1773-5. We may then take the opportunity of comparing the Edicts of Pugachev with governmental Manifestos against him, and then Pugachev's own testimony with the recollections of a contemporaneous noble. Under the impact of the Revolt, Catherine moved to complete the major administrative reform of her reign, the Institution of the Administration of the Provinces of 1775. And ten years later, the Charter of the Nobility, was at the centre of her most important dispensations concerning society. Synopses of these two pieces of legislation bring the collection to a close.

Of course, there are glaring omissions from it, concerning the development of towns and the influence of the French Revolution, for example. There may be an opportunity for rectifying such weaknesses elsewhere. As for the introductions to the documents included here, they are intended to run on from one to another in a manner adding to the cohesion of the collection. However, a certain amount of familiarity is assumed with the rudiments of Russian and European history of the late eighteenth century. It should be remembered that the Russian calendar was by that time eleven days in arrears of that recently introduced into most other states comprising the continent.

This work has taken me much longer than I first expected, nearly ten years on and off, being put aside sometimes for other projects and more than once in despair. For eighteenth-century Russian does not translate easily into English: the sentences can be extremely long, while the syntax and vocabulary are often obscure even for native speakers of the language. The translations that I have finally arrived at are mostly literal, a major exception being administrative terms. Thus, I have rendered *sovestnyi sud* as court of equity rather than of conscience, and *voevoda* as sheriff, for example. Many specialist colleagues will not be happy with these, nor with many other aspects of the translations. Thanking them in advance for their criticisms, and accepting full responsibility for all its inadequacies, I would only ask them to keep the basic purpose of the work in mind. The system of transliteration used is basically that of the *Slavic Review*, deviations including iu- and

-ia rather than yu- and ya-, final -ii instead of -y, and the omission of final soft signs.

A number of sympathisers with the project have generously given it of their time and expertise. I have been particularly fortunate as far as the most difficult (and finally intractable) problem, that of the translation of the Table of Ranks, has been concerned. In the first place, I was helped on several technical points by the late S.M. Troitskii, whose published writings on the subject have formed the basis for the introduction to the Table. Secondly, Brenda Meehan-Waters made a careful reading of a draft translation and offered many suggestions for its improvement. I am also grateful to her for sending me a copy of an unpublished paper on "Social and Career Characteristics of the Russian Elite, 1689-1761" and for giving me notice of a contribution to *California Slavic Studies* by Helju Bennett entitled "Evolution of the Meanings of *Chin*: An Introduction to the Russian Institution of Rank Ordering and Niche Assignment from the Time of Peter the Great's Table of Ranks to the Bolshevik Revolution". Unfortunately, I was not able to see a copy of this article in time to make use of it here, but it is certainly to be recommended as a positive step towards the elucidation of a piece of legislation which puzzled bureaucrats at the time and has baffled scholars since. Brenda Meehan-Waters also corrected some errors in my translations of Tatishchev's *Dissertation* and the Emancipation of the Nobility. Archie Brown kindly checked his translation of Desnitskii's *Proposal* against mine and gave me a list of inaccuracies and infelicities. Dr. Philip Clendenning accelerated the inter-library loan process for me, and provided some useful references. My wife Rosie has given all kinds of help, including proof reading, and the University of Aberdeen has as always been a bountiful source of assistance, from senior, junior and secretarial members of the History and other departments, especially the Russian and from the Library.

It is a happy irony that this undertaking has now become in some ways superfluous for one of its original instigators, Dr. E.N. Williams, who has been adding Russian to his other languages in the interim. Coincidentally, completion has come in the year of his retirement. And so, as well as thanking him again for first making me into an historian, I can take this opportunity of wishing him many peaceful years away from the hurly-burly of teaching and productive of further fine works to join *The Eighteenth-Century Constitution, The Ancien Regime in Europe,* and so on. Included in the dedication is his principal collaborator and wife.

Paul Dukes

King's College,
Old Aberdeen, May 1978

1. The Table of Ranks, 1722

INTRODUCTION

Ranks were instituted in Russia during the medieval period. At first, they were closely tied to office, but later also to blood. They became intimately connected with the Muscovite system of precedence or preferment known as *mestnichestvo,* according to which aristocratic families made claims to appropriate places in the service hierarchy. This system worked well enough in the sixteenth century, but not so well in the seventeenth; it was abolished in 1682, and the records used for its implementation were destroyed. The new arrangements, with five basic ranks, constituted an important part of the late seventeenth-century reorganisation of the bureaucracy. However, the pretensions of the old nobility still persisted and received some recognition, including from Peter I after his accession.

Around the turn of the century, in several neighbouring European states undergoing the process of the entrenchment of absolutism, monarchs promulgated their own "tables of ranks". Peter decided to help consolidate Russian absolutism in a similar manner while eliminating anomalies in the triangular relationship of blood, rank and office. After receiving information and advice from a number of sources, Peter ordered his collaborator A. I. Osterman to prepare a preliminary project towards the implementation of his decision in 1719. The son of a Lutheran pastor from Westphalia and a former student at Jena University who knew Latin, Dutch, French, Russian and German and who had acted for Peter on diplomatic assignments since 1711, Osterman was well equipped for this new task, which occupied much of his time from the end of 1719 to the beginning of 1721.

In his Announcement about Ranks, Osterman omitted the church hierarchy and army and navy officers, concentrating exclusively on court and civil positions, and giving precedence to the court as was customary at that time. While most court ranks listed by Osterman had German names, 34 out of 44 were already in existence in Russia. The rest of the new court ranks were taken from Frederick I of Prussia's arrangement of 1705. Like the court ranks, most of the civil were already set up in Russia by the time Osterman got to work on their compilation. Over 90% of them had appeared in official documents by 1719, many of them having recently come from the Swedish and Danish systems created respectively by Charles XII in 1696 and Christian V in

1699. Osterman used the same German and Scandinavian sources extensively in the fourteen *punkty* or points of explanation which he appended to his Announcement before submitting it to the Emperor.

Peter then subjected the Announcement to a thorough revision. He accepted Osterman's omission of the church hierarchy, for which he had no love. The armed forces were a different matter, and he not only brought them in but gave them precedence, particularly the guards and the artillery. Here again, most of the ranks were already adopted in Russia, many of them in the military and naval regulations of 1716 and 1720, several of them in the earlier regularisation of the army in the reign of Peter's father Aleksei, and at least one of them—*kvartermeister* —in Muscovite records as early as 1632. Peter also listed civil ranks before those of the court, and transferred the *ober-gerol 'dmeister*, the Senior Heraldmaster, from the court column to the civil, a clear indication of his view of the nobility as cadres for service rather than adornments for palaces. He omitted from the preamble Osterman's acknowledgement of his sources, and radically amended the *punkty*, too. Characteristically, he increased the number and severity of threats and punishments. He augmented the number of civil ranks which would carry with them hereditary nobility (from six to eight, as opposed to Christian V of Denmark's three, —"a logical development of the bureaucratic principle of service"[1] in Troitskii's view). And, as a clear demonstration of the pre-eminence of the armed forces, he attributed hereditary nobility to all commissioned officers, that is to all members of the armed forces in the thirteen classes or divisions, or of the draft table.

In early 1721, Peter gave the draft to the senate for its scrutiny, and he ordered the War and Admiralty Colleges to make their comments, too. The senate compared the Table to its nearest equivalents in England, Denmark, Prussia, France and Sweden. It accepted the superiority of the ranks of the armed forces, pointing out "that the order composed for military and naval ranks is comparable to the ranks of sovereigns, particularly the French, as an ancient and autocratic king."[2] At the same time, the senators wanted old ranks such as the boyars to have some recognition, to maintain some of that deference to aristocracy of blood which Peter wanted to discourage. They accepted their own exclusion from the Table as senators, but were anxious that those who sat in the senate should be given a due reward in rank, and that the ranks of chancellor and privy councillor should be raised. The War and Admiralty Colleges were also keen to protect their own, and they agreed with the senate about the recognition of ancient lineage. Peter did not reject such pleas entirely, acknowledging that the old aristocracy could maintain its privileges if it truly served the state. He gave a warmer welcome, however, to the recommendation of his advisers that adequate levels of remuneration should be maintained at all levels of the service hierarchy. A further incentive to competence in his view was the designation of education abroad as a kind of state service which could merit special rewards of rank.

After final top level discussions in early 1722, Peter signed a final draft on 24 January (the date given in the Complete Collection of the Russian Laws), but a few late changes were made, and the Table of Ranks was not published until 14 February 1722. The tsar himself composed the title and, finding thirteen divisions an unsuitable number, added another one, class 11 consisting of a single token function, that of ship's secretary. Peter also made some more forceful personal contributions to the *punkty* or points of explanation, whose number had by now grown from Osterman's original fourteen to nineteen, and which had all been subject to minor or major revision. Undoubtedly, the preparation of the Table had been thorough. In the words of Troitskii:

> "It was characteristic of Peter as a stateman to turn to his collaborators for advice. He was distinguished by a wide outlook and the ability to make important decisions while taking into account the opinions of other people, whether for a plan of implementing a military operation, an important diplomatic step or the preparation of a new law."[3]

The situation regarding rank in Austria, Venice, Spain and Poland was closely studied as well as in those states already mentioned, Denmark, Sweden and Prussia becoming most influential. Domestic precedent as well as foreign example was used. If it was a graft of the most modern administrative and command systems available, the recipient had for fifty years or more been undergoing the preparation necessary for the graft to take. Had this not been the case, the Table of Ranks would not have proved as durable and adaptable as it did, surviving in its essentials to the Revolution of 1917 and in some senses perhaps beyond.

In the final version, 262 duties are distributed in vertical columns among the fourteen divisions: 126 (48%) come from the armed forces; 94 (36%) are civil; and 42 (16%) are connected with the court. The armed forces are separated into the land forces, guards, artillery and navy, with the guards receiving a two-rank bonus as a mark of their distinguished position (a guards colonel being equal with a major-general from the land forces, and so on). From the civil column were omitted lower-level bureaucrats (*kantseliaristy*, *podkantseliaristy*, *kopiisty* and *pisty* — clerks, sub-clerks, copyists and scribes), and some high ranks, old and new. These included firstly, boyars and other Muscovite titles indissolubly mixed with the idea of an aristocracy of blood, and secondly, "viceroys" and "privy councillors" and suchlike as found in certain European states, officials who could exercise a certain amount of independence from the main body of the state apparatus. (*Tainyi sovetnik*, although translated here as "privy councillor", was, like all other Russian officials, fully incorporated into the state bureaucracy.) Included in the civil column were not only state bureaucrats but also town functionaries, professors of the academy, specialists in mining and forestry, archivists and translators. As for the officials of the court, they too were encouraged to join in the pursuit of rewards in rank for state service, forgetting the old Muscovite seclusion and exclusive privileges.

The final version of the *punkty* or points of explanation gave emphasis to several of the policies already indicated in the arrangement of the Table itself, as well as in earlier discussion: particularly, the supremacy of service, the seniority of the armed forces, and the overall predominance of the nobility. For example, firstly, *punkt* 1 was number 12 in earlier drafts. Its promotion was probably intended to underline the necessity for everybody, even for "Princes from Our blood", to be included in the hierarchy of ranks received from the state in return for some contribution to its prosperity. In *punkt* 8, Peter made in clear that "We do not allow anybody rank, until they have rendered service to Us and the fatherland". And *punkt* 17 made clear the distinction as well as the inter-dependence between serving rank and function, with implications for others besides those listed in it. The seniority of the armed forces was made clear enough in the preamble, and in *punkty* 13 and 15. Peter did not want to make arrangements in rank which would be "outrageous to military people who have received it after many years of cruel service;"[4] and he confirmed to the armed forces hereditary nobility in all fourteen divisions, as opposed to the top eight in the civil and court columns. The wives and children of serving nobles were to receive commensurate privileges; the sons were especially favoured, as Junkers or cadets *(punkty* 13 and 14). The predominance of the nobility was to be protected by the newly-appointed Heraldmaster, as described in *punkt* 16, checking credentials and awarding coats-of-arms to all properly qualified, including nobles of old lineage who had not served. As always, Peter reinforced his commands by the threat of condign punishment (*punkty* 3 and 13) and the imposition of strict control, whether by the police Fiscals (*punkty* 3 and 13) or by severe sumptuary regulations (*punkt* 19).

As we shall see, the Table of Ranks was subjected to several changes during the course of the eighteenth century. Some of the very terms employed in it declined in use, among them *rang* itself. Changes, as well as anomalies and contradictions, confront the translator with overwhelming problems and no satisfactory solution. For the sake of inner consistency, I have in the following always rendered *rang* as "rank", and *chin* as "grade". In later documents, with *rang* fallen into comparative desuetude, I shall resume the translation of *chin* as "rank".

It would be even more difficult to give an English rendering of all the terms used in the Table, particularly since many of them are of Central European origin. Both the difficulty of such a translation and the flavour of the Table might be suggested by the following transliteration of the lowest rank, 14 in the court column: Nadvornoi Ustavshchik. Gofmeister Pazhev. Gof Sekretar. Nadvornoi Bibliotekar. Antikvarius. Nadvornoi Kamerir. Nadvornoi Auditor. Nadvornoi Kvartirmeister. Nadvornoi Aptekar. Shlos Fokht. Nadvornoi Tseigmeister. Kabinet Kureiry. Mundshenk. Kukhenmeister. Keller-Meister. Ekzertsiitsiimeister. Nadvornoi Barbir. Realising the insurmountable problem of putting these and all the others into English after several vain attempts, and comforted by the circumstance that many fell into disuse before the accession of Catherine II as some others were added, I have finally decided to give just the following abstract of the Table. In the original, it is set out in parallel columns after the first sentence.

MILITARY

Land forces. Class 1. General-Fieldmarshal. 2. Generals of the Cavalry and Infantry. 3. Lieutenant-Generals. 4. Major-Generals. 5. Brigadiers. 6. Colonels. 7. Lieutenant-Colonels. 8. Majors. 9. Captains. 10. Lieutenant-Captains. 11. —. 12. Lieutenants. 13. Second-Lieutenants. 14. Ensigns.

Guards. Class 1. —. 2. —. 3. —. 4. Colonel. 5. Lieutenant-Colonels. 6. Majors. 7. Captains. 8. Lieutenant-Captains. 9. Lieutenants. 10. Second-Lieutenants. 11. —. 12. Ensigns. 13. —. 14. —.

Artillery. Class 1. —. 2. General. 3. Lieutenant-General. 4. Major-General. 5. Colonels. 6. Lieutenant-Colonels. 7. Majors. 8. Captains. 9. Lieutenant-Captains. 10. Lieutenants. 11. —. 12. Second-Lieutenants. 13. Junkers. 14. Ensigns.

Navy. Class 1. General-Admiral. 2. Admirals. 3. Vice-Admirals. 4. Rear-Admirals. 5. Commanders. 6. Captains of the First Rank. 7. Captains of the Second Rank. 8. Captains of the Third Rank. 9. Lieutenant-Captains. 10. Lieutenants. 11. Ship's Secretaries. 12. Second-Lieutenants. 13. —. 14. Ship's Commissars.

CIVIL

Class 1. Chancellor. 2. Actual Privy Councillors. 3. Procurator-General. 4. College Presidents. Privy Councillors. 5. Heraldmaster. 6. College Procurators. 7. Senior Secretaries of the War, Admiralty and Foreign Affairs Colleges. 8. Senior Secretaries of the Other Colleges. 9. Titular Councillor. Secretaries of the War, Admiralty and Foreign Affairs Colleges. 10. Secretaries of the Other Colleges. 11. —. 12. Legal and

Provincial Secretaries. 13. County Secretaries. 14. College Commissars.

COURT
Class 1. –. 2. Senior Marshal. 3. Senior Stablemaster. 4. Senior Chamberlain. 5. Chamberlain. 6. Stablemaster. 7. Chamberlain of H.R.H. the Empress. 8. Titular Chamberlains. 9. Court Master of Ceremonies. 10. –. 11. –. 12. Court Junkers. 13. –. 14. Court Butler.

Such an abstract not only condenses but simplifies. It lists service titles much more than offices or functions. This, it is true, indicates the direction that Russian bureaucrats themselves were to take as they wrestled with the anomalies and contradictions of the original Table of Ranks throughout the eighteenth and nineteenth centuries. Scholars today may be pardoned for finding it still a source of confusion and anxiety, but its essential purpose was and remains clear enough: in the words of Brenda Meehan-Waters, "The Table of Ranks was a means for the giving of nobility to those who had none via the achievement of rank, and the giving of rank to those who already had nobility."[5]

Footnotes*

1. S.M. Troitskii, "Iz istorii", p.103
2. *Ibid.,* p.106.
3. S.M. Troitskii, *Russkii absoliutizm,* p.110.
4. *Ibid.,* p.106.
5. Brenda Meehan-Waters in an unpublished paper, "Social and Career Characteristics of the Russian Elite, 1689-1761".

*Full author-title entries are found in the bibliography at the back (pp.173-6).

The Table of Ranks
Complete Collection of the Laws of the Russian Empire, First Series,
Volume 6, pp. 486-493, No. 3890, 24 January 1722.

The Table of Ranks of all grades, Military, Civil and Court, which grades are in which class; and those which are in one class, they have seniority among themselves according to the time of entry into the grade, however Military are higher than the others, even though [latter] promoted into that class first . . . [The Table of Ranks]. To the table of ranks, instituted as set out above are appended these points, how everybody must act with regard to these ranks.

1.   Princes *[Printsy]* who originate from Our blood and those who are married to Our Princesses have on all occasions precedence and rank over all princes *[kniaz'ia]* and high servants of the Russian State.

2.   Naval officers are appointed to commands with land officers in the following manner: when they have the same rank, the naval officer commands the land officer at sea, and the land officer commands the naval officer on land, irrespective of seniority in grade.

3.   Whoever shall demand honour higher than his rank, or take a place higher than the rank given him, shall be fined two months pay for each offence; and if he serves without pay, then let him pay a fine equal to the pay of those grades which are of the same rank, and actually receive pay; a third of the fine money to be given to the informer, and the rest to be used in hospitals. But this observance of each rank is not demanded on such occasions as when good friends or neighbours get together, or in public assemblies, but only in churches during Divine Service, in Court ceremonies such as ambassadorial audiences, formal dinners, official meetings, weddings, christenings, and suchlike public festivity and business; a similar fine is obligatory for him who gives a place to somebody lower than his rank, which the Fiscals must carefully watch for, so that enthusiasm for service might be encouraged, and honour given to those in service, and not to louts and parasites: the above fine to be levied for offences on both the male and female sex.

4.   The same fine for him who demands a rank, when he cannot show the patent appropriate for his grade.

5.   Moreover, nobody must assume rank according to the character reference that he received in foreign service, until We have confirmed that character reference, which confirmation We, to each in accordance with his services, will gladly grant.

6.   Without a patent, release from service will give nobody a rank, unless such release will be given by Our hand.

7.   All married women occupy ranks according to the grades of their husbands, and when they act in a manner contrary to this they must pay

a fine such as their husbands would have paid for the same offence.

8. Although We allow free entry before others of lower grade in public assembly where the Court is to be found to the sons of the Russian State's Princes, Counts, Barons, distinguished Nobility, and servants of the highest rank, because of their aristocratic birth, or because of the outstanding grades of their fathers, and although We keenly desire to see that they are distinguished from others according to their dignity in all cases; however We do not allow anybody rank, until they have rendered service to Us and the fatherland, and have received a character reference to this effect.

9. On the other hand all maidens whose fathers are in the first rank, until they are married will receive rank over all wives who are to be found in rank 5, that is, lower than Major-General, but higher than Brigadier; and maidens, whose fathers are in rank 2, over wives who are in rank 6, that is lower than Brigadier but higher than Colonel; and maidens, whose fathers are in rank 3, over wives of rank 7, that is lower than Lieutenant-Colonel, and as for others, as ranks ordain.

10. Ladies and Maidens in attendance at Court while they are actually in grades, should receive the following ranks:

The Supreme Chief Lady of the Household *[Ober-Gofmeisterina]* of Her Majesty the Sovereign Empress, has a rank over all Ladies.

Actual Ladies-in-Waiting *[Stats-Damy]* of Her Majesty the Sovereign Empress, follow after the wives of Actual Privy Councillors.

Actual Chamber-Maidens *[Kamer-Devitsy]* , have a rank with wives of College Presidents.

Household Ladies *[Gof-Damy]* , with wives of Brigadiers.

Household Maidens *[Gof-Devitsy]* , with wives of Colonels.

The Chief Lady of the Household *[Gofmeisterina]* of Our Tsarevnas, with Actual Ladies-in-Waiting of Her Highness the Empress.

Chamber-Maidens of their Highnesses the Tsarevnas follow after the Household Ladies of Her Majesty the Sovereign Empress.

The Household Maidens of their Highnesses the Tsarevnas follow after the Household Maidens of H.M. the Sovereign Empress.

11. All Russian or foreign servants who are or actually were in the first eight ranks, their lawful children and descendants in perpetuity are considered equal to the best ancient Nobility in all honours and advantages, even though they are of low birth, and have never been promoted to Noble rank by Crowned Heads or granted coats of arms.

12. When any of Our high or low servants actually has two grades or more, or has received a rank higher than the grade that he actually occupies: he shall in all cases have the rank of the higher grade. But when he is carrying out his duties in the lower grade, then he cannot be in the place of his higher rank or title, but according to the grade that he actually holds.

13. Since civil grades were not arranged formerly, and almost nobody

11

or very few from the Nobility earned higher rank from below in the proper manner; and absolute necessity now exists for higher grades: for this reason take who is suitable, even if he has had no grade. But since from the point of view of rank this will be outrageous to military people who have received it after many years of cruel service and see those who have not served equal or superior to themselves: therefore whoever receives a grade must earn the rank over an appropriate number of years in the proper manner. Therefore henceforth give to the Chief Fiscal the names and dates of appointment of those who have been put into a civil place from below by the Senate in an irregular manner because of present need, so that the Fiscals can see that they perform in ranks according to this decree. And so that henceforth vacancies can be taken up not on the side but in a regular manner, as is carried on in military ranks: therefore in the Civil Colleges, there must be 6 or 7 Junkers of the College, or less; and if more are necessary, then this must be reported.

14. The children of the Nobility must be promoted in the Colleges from below. Specifically: firstly Junkers in the Colleges, if they are proficient, and examined by the College, and presented in the Senate, and have received patents; and those who have not become proficient, but have been taken on for lack of those who have: these should first be enrolled as Titular Junkers of the College, and those who do not have ranks up to Actual Junker of a College should remain without ranks for these years:

		Years	Months
As against:	Corporal	1	—
	Sergeant	1	—
	Ensign	1	6
	Lieutenant	2	—
	Captain	2	—
	Major	2	—
	Lieutenant-Colonel	2	—
	Colonel	3	6

The terms of corporal and sergeant to be counted for those who have studied and really learned what is necessary for Collegial administration. Specifically, everything concerned with justice, also the external and internal trade of the Empire and the Economy, in which they must be examined. Let some of those who have learned the aforementioned subjects be sent from the Colleges abroad, for practice of the subject. And those who make outstanding contributions may be promoted for their labour to higher ranks, as is done for those who show particular zeal in the military service, but this to be done in the Senate only, and with Our signature.

15. To military men of commoner origin who serve up to Commissioned rank, when one of them receives the aforementioned grade, he is a Noble and so are the children born while he holds the Commission. But if there are henceforth no children, but there were before, and the father petitions, then Nobility may be given to one son only on whose behalf the father has made a request. Other grades, both civil and court, who are in ranks but are not from the Nobles, their children are not Nobles.

16. And because it is given to nobody except Us and other Crowned Heads to grant the honour of Nobility with coat of arms and seal, and nevertheless it has often been the case that certain persons call themselves Nobles, but are not really Nobles, others have wilfully taken coats of arms, which their ancestors did not have, neither from Our ancestors nor from foreign Crowned Heads, and moreover have the temerity sometimes to take such a coat of arms as reigning Monarchs and other outstanding families actually possess: therefore to those whom this concerns We thus graciously point out that everybody should henceforth beware of such an unseemly action and of the consequent dishonour and penalty. It is announced to all that for this matter We have appointed a Heraldmaster, and thus everybody must come to him for this matter and give reports and ask for decisions in the proper manner: that is, those who have Nobility and a coat of arms for it to prove that they or their ancestors had from some grant either from Our ancestors or by Our bounty been brought to this honour. If somebody cannot prove it immediately and definitely he should be given one and a half years; and then he must definitely prove it, and if he does not prove it, (and say why exactly) this should be reported to the Senate; and having been considered in the Senate, reported to Us.

If some ask about an award for conspicuous services, then enquire about the services, and if any of them turn out to be actually deserving, report this to the Senate and the Senate should make representations to Us. And whoever has served up to commissioned rank, Russian or foreigner, from the Nobility: give them coats of arms according to their services. And those who have not been in military service, and have not deserved anything, but can demonstrate not less than a hundred years [of nobility]: give coats of arms to them too. Foreign people in service have either by their diplomas, or by official testimony from the government of their fatherland, to prove their Nobility and coats of arms.

17. Moreover the grades listed below, to wit: Presidents and Vice-Presidents in District Courts, [Prezidenty and Vitse-Prezidenty in Nadvornye Sudy], Senior Attorneys in the Capital [Ober-landrikhtery in the Rezidentsiia], The President in the Magistracy [Magistrat] in the Capital, Senior Commissars in the Colleges, Sheriffs [voevody], Senior Treasurers [Ober-Rentmeistery], and Attorneys in the Provinces

13

and Counties, The Treasurer of Monetary Affairs, Directors of Customs in the ports, Senior Commissars of the Economy in the Provinces, Collectors [Kameriry] in the Colleges, Councillors [Ratmany] in the Capital, Post-Masters, Commissars in the Colleges, Collectors in the Provinces, Local [Zemskie] Commissars, Assessors [Assessory] in Provincial Courts, Local Treasurers, cannot be considered as permanent grades, but rather as established functions [za uriad], so for those listed above and their like: because they are not grades: therefore they must have rank, while they are actually at their affairs. And when they change positions or retire, then they do not have that rank.

18. Those who have been dismissed for serious crimes, publicly punished on the square, or even only stripped naked [and punished], or tortured, these are to be deprived of the title and rank that they have, unless for certain services their honour has been wholly restored by Us with Our own hand and seal: and there will be a public announcement about this.

Interpretation [of the law] concerning those tortured
During torture it happens that many miscreants cite others through spite: therefore, whoever has been wrongfully tortured cannot be included among the dishonoured, but he must be given Our charter with the circumstance of his innocence.

19. Since also the prominence and worthiness of the grade of any individual is often diminished, when the dress and other behaviour are not consonant with them, similarly on the other hand many are ruined, when they have accoutrements higher than their grade and property: We therefore graciously point out that everybody should have the dress, equipage and livery as his position and character reference demand. All must act in this manner, and must beware of the ordained penalty and greatest punishment.

2. V.N. Tatishchev, The Voluntary and Agreed Dissertation of the Assembled Russian Nobility about the State Government, c.1730

INTRODUCTION

Attempting to interpret the evolution of the Table of Ranks in the years following the death of Peter the Great, the historian would do well to heed the following wise words of M.M. Bogoslovskii, written though they originally were in another connection:

"He who would describe this activity limiting himself to the systematic and multifaceted programme set out above, would very much recall that newspaper reporter who gave a review of a concert which did not take place after reading the bill."[1]

To give just one illustration of the gap between intention and reality as far as the Table was concerned, the Heraldmaster confessed himself still incapable in 1767 of fulfilling the instructions which had first been given to his predecessor in 1722. A register of the whole nobility should have been compiled, but, "up to now accurate information on nobles and their children, in service and retired, also deceased and newly born, has not yet been received from all regions."[2] And doubts persisted in the Heraldmaster's mind about the qualifications for nobility: was it to be achieved by service rank, possession of an estate, or both? In its instruction to the Legislative Commission of 1767, the Heraldmaster's Office asked for a clearer ruling on this problem, as well as on that of the ennoblement of those reaching military *ober-ofitserstvo* (rank 14) or civil *ober-sekretarstvo* (rank 8). The senate, Russia's highest administrative body, confessed in its instruction to the Commission that it shared the doubts of the Heralds concerning qualifications for nobility. If responsible officials of the 1760s were uncertain about the exact specifications of the Table of Ranks, there can be little wonder that later historians have also been puzzled about them.

There was certainly some consolidation of the bureaucracy and further regularisation of the armed forces during the period from the death of Peter the Great in 1725 to the accession of Catherine II in 1762. But considerably more noticeable has been the manipulation of patronage by successive governments brought to power by a series of palace revolutions and acting not so much according to "the authority of state institutions" as "the power of persons". The responsibility for this unhappy situation lay partly with Peter the Great, who had proclaimed in 1722 that henceforth the Russian monarch would choose his own heir, but then himself died without doing so. His widow was acclaimed by the establishment, but the Empress Catherine had much more taste for drink than command, and allowed one of Peter's henchmen, Prince A.D. Menshikov, to take over much of her autocracy. At first, Menshikov managed to dominate the Supreme Privy Council set up in 1726 as an intermediary between the sovereign and the administration. He hoped to secure his power further through the marriage of his daughter Maria to the heir apparent, Peter's grandson, also called Peter. Dissipation carried off Catherine in 1727 before the wedding, and Menshikov had to struggle to retain his predominance. Realising that with successors to thrones as with other forms of property, possession was nine points of the law, he guarded the eleven-year-old Peter II closely in his own house, keeping away regents designated by Catherine. But he was soon out-manoeuvred, and sent off into exile in the late summer of 1727. The principal usurpers of his power were the brothers Dolgorukii, who dominated a reconstructed Supreme Privy Council, whose members were all given precedence over full generals in a decree of 1728. The Dolgorukiis intended that one of their daughters, the Princess Catherine, would succeed where Maria Menshikov had failed. But in January 1730 on the very day appointed for the nuptials in Moscow, to which the Dolgorukiis had returned the court (somewhat appropriately since one of their ancestors was considered to be the founder of the old capital) the young Emperor Peter II died of smallpox. As at the death of the first Peter, no heir had been designated, and so a crisis over the successor ensued.

The Supreme Privy Council offered the job to Anna of Courland, a daughter of Peter the Great's half-brother and co-tsar, Ivan V. But the offer was made with eight "Conditions" devised by Prince D. M. Golitsyn, a close associate of the Dolgorukiis. Without the approval of the Supreme Privy Council, Anna was not to make war or peace, impose new taxes or make important promotions, take away the life, honour or property of a noble without a trial, grant estates or villages, appoint a Russian or a foreigner to a court office, or spend state income. Anna at first accepted the Conditions, but as news of them leaked out they were not given much of a welcome by the nobles already assembled in Moscow for the wedding. In a welter of alarms and excursions, the Supreme Privy Council decided to ask their fellow-members of the ruling class to put forward their own views on appropriate measures to take in the critical situation then obtaining. There were about a dozen acceptances of this invitation, by far the most articulate of them being "The Voluntary and Agreed Dissertation and Opinion of the Assembled Russian Nobility about the State Government", composed by V.N. Tatishchev.

Tatishchev was a man of many parts. Born a noble in 1686 in the city of Pskov or surrounding district the young Vasilii Nikitich joined the army early in the eighteenth century, and saw service in the campaign of the Pruth at the battle of Poltava and elsewhere before entering in 1716 the Moscow Artillery School under Field Marshal Jacob Bruce, an outstanding expert in artillery and engineering. As well as having considerable experience in these fields, Tatishchev had also in 1712 been sent abroad, particularly to Prussia, to study them and other military affairs. His interests had already come to include history, geography and languages. A mature student of distinction, Tatishchev was soon given by Bruce and Peter the Great a number of assignments connected with his specialities, in St. Petersburg, the Baltic Provinces and Germany. In 1718, Tatishchev helped Bruce in his duties as President of the newly-formed College of Mines and Manufactures and as one of the leading negotiators at the Aland Congress attempting to bring to an end the Great Northern War with Sweden. A project of his own concerning a land survey deepened his interest in Russian geography and history, and he devoted what little time he could spare to such pursuits during the years from 1720 to 1724 which he spent mostly on state service in the Urals, directing the development of mines and metallurgical establishments there. Surviving charges of bribery and corruption, Tatishchev next went to Sweden on a mission with several aims, including arrangements for Russians to go to train as mining engineers and metallurgists. As ever, he kept up his interests in the humanities, making the acquaintance of Swedish historians and of their work on early Russia.

Back in Russia in 1726 after the death of Peter the Great, Tatishchev was again under suspicion of monetary misconduct, particularly of squandering valuable funds on historical materials. Again the charges did not stick, but nevertheless the next few years were not the happiest either for Tatishchev or for two other devotees of the Petrine reforms, who formed with him the "Learned Guard", one of the first Russian circles for the discussion and propagation of the ideas of the early Enlightenment. Apart from Tatishchev himself, the members were Archbishop Feofan Prokopovich of Novgorod and Prince A.D. Kantemir. All three were undoubtedly learned, familiar not only with much of classical writing and religious teaching, but also with Russian history and recent European thought. They were thoroughly at home with concepts such as "reason", the "social contract" and "natural law", which they had imbued from such authorities as Boyle, Hobbes and Locke, Leibniz and Wolff, Pufendorf and Grotius. Yet, as Marc Raeff has aptly argued, "From the social and economic points of view, Russia was closer to most German states then to the more advanced trading and manufacturing Holland or England or the immensely wealthy France,"[3] and so the "Learned Guard", tended to be German rather than Dutch, English or French in their intellectual orientation. And of all the German influences, the most important was Christian Wolff, the Pietist. Not only were Wolff and his pupils earnest proselytisers, they and many of their learned fellow-countrymen were under some pressure to look for work away from home because of the unfavourable economic, political and cultural climate prevailing there. Moreover, Marc Raeff tells us, there were more profound reasons for the affinity which such men as the members of the "Learned Guard" felt for the teachings of Wolff and his associates at the beginning of the eighteenth century:

> "In the first place was their sincere and complete acceptance of Christian doctrine and the injunction to obey constituted authorities, an attitude most welcome to a monarch jealous of his absolute power. No less significant a factor was the Wolffian interpretation of the natural law. It stressed the conceptions of obligation and duty as the prerequisite of individual rights, in contrast to the 'possessive individualism' of the Hobbesian and Lockean tradition. It also gave priority to the community and to social institutions over and against the claims of the autonomous individual, as emphasised by the English and French notions of natural rights. Such an orientation, buttressed by a strong belief in neo-stoicism which assigned a major role to human will and activity within the framework of generally valid universal moral laws, appealed to a service-oriented society dedicated to total change of traditional circumstances. The doctrines taught by Wolff and his followers gave moral and philosophic sanction to the goal-directed, wilful, active state and administration that Peter the Great had rooted in Russia."[4]

Somewhat suspect in the eyes of the Supreme Privy Council, the members of the "Learned Guard" still managed to discuss and put forward such views in the years immediately following their master's death.

Tatishchev in particular had something of a reputation among his contemporaries as an atheist. In reality, like many other savants of the eighteenth century, he was more of a deist, recognising the omnipotence of a Supreme Being and the truths of Holy Writ but paying little respect to the established church or to many of its practitioners. He abhorred the exploitation of the credulity and superstition of the people, yet at the same time believed that religion properly inculcated would keep the people from vice and crime. Tatishchev himself claimed that he was not much of a philosopher, and professed a practical view of knowledge, which was to be used to help man to achieve self-awareness and self-perfection. He took full opportunity of expressing such attitudes in his "Dissertation", where "reason", the "social contract" and "natural law" are all employed for the specific purpose of establishing the autocracy of Anna, as are classical ideas such as Aristotle's three forms of government and arguments drawn not only from classical times but also from Russian and European history and geography. Tatishchev's "scientific" approach in general and his particular argument that "great and spacious states with many envious neighbours" could not be governed except by autocracy exerted considerable influence on later eighteenth-century writers, including in all probability the great Montesquieu himself. Some of his fellow-countrymen, including his two colleagues in the "Learned Guard", anticipated some of his ideas, notably Prokopovich in his "Right of the Monarch's Will". And yet there is a very strong case for calling the "Dissertation" the first mature modern piece of Russian political thought.

Much of it appears to have been written after Anna had torn up the "Conditions" of the Supreme Privy Council and firmly established her own autocracy. A Soviet scholar G.A. Protasov has persuasively argued that "The project does not appear to be a document of the actions of the nobility during the events of 1730; it is the result of the later understanding of the author's notes on the nobility's plans in the period".[5] Yet at least the ten suggestions were written in 1730, it would seem. Tatishchev certainly found time during his later career to work on this and other projects, notably his multi-volumed Russian history. He was entrusted with more state commissions in the Urals and elsewhere; he was also held under suspicion by successive governments, dismissed from service and even imprisoned. But he somehow contrived to die peacefully in bed on his estate near Moscow in 1750.

Footnotes

1. Quoted by S.M. Troitskii, *Russkii absoliutizm*, p.38.
2. P. Dukes, *Catherine the Great*, p.145.
3. M. Raeff, "The Enlightenment", p.36.
4. *Ibid.*, p.35.
5. Quoted by R.L. Daniels, *V.N. Tatishchev*, p.39.

The Voluntary and Agreed Dissertation and opinion of the Assembled Russian Nobility about the State Government.

The Supreme Privy Council, in its announcement about the death of Peter II, jointly announced the election to the throne of the Tsarevna Anna Ioannovna, Duchess of Courland. And although they asked the then assembled top four ranks [*generalitet*] if they were agreed with the election, they had however already violated the appropriate procedure of elections because this is not the announcement of a proper succession, but an election, and of such a kind that there has not been from the foundation of the Russian State. Although there have been three elections, that is of Tsar Boris Godunov, Vasilii Shuiskii and Mikhail Romanov, all of them had no sequel. And the first two elections were faulty because they were improperly carried out; in the first there was compulsion, in the second perfidy. And according to natural law the election must be with the agreement of all subjects, some personally, others through trustees, as such a procedure is sanctioned in many states, and not by four or five individuals, as has now been carried out most improperly. And although in the Roman or the German Empire, it was enacted that seven and now nine electors [*kurfirsty*] should elect the emperor, we have no such law and must not follow that of others. And moreover we must especially understand, that in this way the electors grew so powerful that the emperor [*Kaiser*] no longer had any power, and they themselves became the sovereigns; and as they were often not in agreement, so the empire grew successively smaller; and the neighbours consequently grew stronger, tearing off parts on all sides; consequently, we cannot expect anything better. This election only is tacitly accepted, because the whole people is satisfied with the person of Her Highness and nobody disputes it. But it must be disputed as a precedent and a law must be composed for such an unexpected situation, so that no disorder should follow, particularly since by such perfidious election as that of Vasilii Shiuskii the whole state was brought into confusion and extreme ruin.

Secondly, and much more seriously: They have dared by themselves to abolish autocracy, and, to introduce aristocracy, announcing to us Her Majesty's letter and points as if she by her own will made them. And they have forced us under the guise of obedience to confirm them with our signatures, as if we approved of their manifest temerity. And as they ceasing that compulsion, have announced: if anybody has anything against what they are presenting, they should tell them about it. And since as shown above, they have improperly and wilfully taken power to themselves, ignoring the worthiness and welfare of the whole nobility [*shliakhetstvo*] and other dignitaries, so it is our duty and necessary obligation to consider carefully and to put forward what should be to the state's benefit and to defend its law as much as possible, neither sinking into inaction nor even more losing our courage so that they should not attempt greater impropriety, seeing us negligent.

In consideration of which the following are the most important circumstances:

(1) At the death of an heirless sovereign, who should command authority over the people?

(2) Who in such a case may change an old law or custom and make a new one?

(3) If it is necessary to change our ancient autocratic form of government, then should it first be discussed, which is the best for the condition of the people and the situation?

(4) Who should make this arrangement and by what procedure?

Dissertation

To the first. We swear allegiance and pledge obedience only to a sovereign who has been elected to the throne or inherited it, and take away his power of legislation at his death, which both frees him from power and his subjects from their oath. He gives others power in government to assist him, and they are right worthy of that honour, power and advantage. However, all this ends with his death and their power ceases, and the people remain generally equal in their former situation, and nobody has the slightest power over anybody else, until the next sovereign confirms them or dismissing them appoints others. Nevertheless, so that the necessary justice and government are not severed, the whole people [obshchenarodie] gives them only that power, which they had by the former laws, and they cannot demand any more from the people without a specific direction.

To the second. It is clear from the above statement that the power of legislation is given only to the sovereign himself. And we have no example of a sovereign giving up that power to anybody, unless he proclaims the heir to the throne and a co-ruler, as was the case in the Roman Empire. However, he allows various confidants to make laws, although without his confirmation not one is effective, because all laws issue from his name. When there is no sovereign, neither his permission nor his confirmation exists, and so nothing can be promulgated in his name. Consequently nobody can change any law or procedure except by agreement of the whole people.

To the third [and fourth]. There is no necessity for a change of government or benefit in it, but rather great harm. But so that this might be clearer, let us examine all regular governments, and then those that are mixed: (1) monarchy or autocracy; (2) aristocracy or an elected government; (3) democracy or popular government. Each region chooses from these various governments, considering the position of the place, the size of the domain and the condition of the people, and not each of these is suitable everywhere, or each government useful. For example: in single cities, or very small regions, where all householders may quickly gather together, here democracy may be profitably adopted, and in a large region it is no longer suitable. In regions which consist of several cities, but are secure from enemy attacks, such as islands and so on, aristocracy might be useful, especially if the people is enlightened by education and applies itself to the maintenance of the laws without compulsion — there such a strict supervision and cruel terror are not necessary.

Great and spacious states with many envious neighbours cannot be ruled by any of those mentioned above, particularly where the people is insufficiently enlightened by education and keeps the law through terror, and not from good conduct, or knowledge of good and evil. In such nothing else is possible but autocracy *[samo-* or *edinovlastie]*. But since the condition of regions varies a lot, their governments are chosen from a mixture of two or all three in parts. Here are examples: Holland, Switzerland, Genoa and so on are all governed on the whole by democracy and call themselves republics. Venice almost alone is governed by aristocracy. Spain, France, Russia, and since olden days Turkey, Persia, India, China, are great states, and cannot be governed otherwise than by autocracy. Then there are the mixtures. The German Empire and Poland are governed by monarchy and aristocracy. England and Sweden consist of all three, as in England the lower parliament or chamber, in Sweden the seim, represent the whole people; the upper parliament, in Sweden the senate — the aristocracy.

Even these cases are insufficient since Rome before the emperors was governed by aristocracy and democracy, and in the case of a serious war elected a dictator and gave him full autocracy. Equally Holland in a difficult situation elected a stadtholder with full authority and England in former times gave the king temporary full authority for certain purposes. From this we see, that old-established republics introduce monarchy on dangerous and difficult occasions, although only temporarily, clearly seeing, that monarchical government is more useful.

We may now consider, which of these three governments, according to the condition of our state, is most useful.

Firstly, democracy cannot be in any way used, because the great size of the state prohibits it. Aristocracy has taught us enough of the harm connected with it; for this it is necessary to remember the historical past.

We do not have our own history before Riurik, but Greek, Roman and northern ancient writers sufficiently fill the gap, calling our ancestors Scythians, and recounting that they had autocratic sovereigns. From Riurik we can see according to our own histories. Up to Mstislav the Great there was complete autocracy *[edinovlastilet'stvo]*, and for no more as in two hundred and fifty years our state spread everywhere, moving its boundaries up to the Danube, the Bug, the Vistula, the Neman and so on. The people were sufficiently enlightened by education; by commerce in Greece, to the north and up to the Caspian Sea it was sufficiently enriched. By the upkeep of sufficient forces they were terrible to all neighbours, who assiduously sought the Russian alliance, as is testified by the history of the Greeks, Hungarians, Poles and German kings, to the considerable benefit and honour of the state. They allied themselves in marriage, with eastern and western emperors, with the kings of France, Hungary, Norway, Sweden, Poland, as our and their histories affirm.

As soon as the grand dukes started to share equally among their children, those who had received shares *[udel'nye]* did not obey the grand dukes, and introduced aristocracy, and then ruined each other through disagreement. The grand dukes became powerless, then the Tartars invaded and seized everything. The Lithuanians tore off a large part of the state which had previously been under their authority. And so the state was enslaved by the Tartars for more than two hundred years.

Ivan the Great dared to eradicate that aristocracy. Gathering together many principalities, he more or less restored monarchy and strengthened it not only to overthrow the power of the Tartars, but also for him or his son to take back many lands from them and from Lithuania. And so the state got back its former honour and security, which lasted until the death of Godunov.

With the overthrow of the False Dmitrii, the perfidious election of Shuiskii and the envy of Golitsyn and others led to a new dissipation. To take to the sovereign a declaration *[zapis']* which seized all power from the sovereign and stole it for themselves, was similar to the present situation. But what came of it? The extreme ruin of the state. The Poles and Swedes tore off many ancient Russian frontiers and took possession of them.

Although the election of tsar Mikhail Fedorovich was properly by the whole people, it was with the same sort of declaration, according to which he could not do anything; but he was happy with the peace.

Tsar Aleksei Mikhailovich, getting the opportunity to lead his troops in Poland and getting back in this way some of his autocracy, restored many of the frontiers from Poland. And if the power-loving Patriarch Nikon had not prevented him, the state would of course have obtained more benefit from his autocracy.

Peter the Great intensified all this, and with his autocracy, brought greater honour, fame and benefit to himself and the state than his forefathers, as all the world may testify. And thus, every reasonable

23

person may sufficiently see, how autocratic government is more useful for us than all others, and the others are dangerous. But have we not seen with an autocratic, but young monarch remote from internal government, that Mazepa possessing great power in fact and Gagarin in intention dared to lead subjects astray? If anybody argues that autocratic government is very burdensome – *First)* to give great power over all the people to one man is unsafe; because however wise, just, gentle and diligent he is, he cannot be faultless and omnicompetent; the more so in that when he gives way to his passions, outrageous unjust violence and ruin are visited upon the innocent, and he insatiably collects property for himself. *Second)* When he chooses a favourite, then that person is equally autocratic and ruins out of envy more than others, particularly if, lowborn or foreign, he hates, persecutes and ruins particularly the elite and those who have served the state. *Third)* The secret chancellery devised by the violent tsar Ivan Vasil'evich [brought] shame and defamation on to reasonable people, and ruin to the state; because for one carelessly said word they torture and execute and deprive guiltless people of their property.

Recalling their exact words, I say in rejoinder:

To the first). Although of course each man is fallible, however sovereigns have advisers, choosing them from reasonable, clever and diligent people. And as he, as lord in his own house, wants to rule it in the best manner, so he has no reason to put his mind to the ruin of his patrimony, but all the more wants to keep it in good order for his children and to increase it. If there should happen to be such a thoughtless person that he neither comprehends what is beneficial, nor takes the advice of wise men and does harm, then he will receive God's punishment. But it would not be sensible to change the former order for such an extraordinary situation. Who can affirm if we see some noble, senselessly destroying his household, that the whole nobility should have its freedom to rule taken away, and be made slaves, knowing that nobody would confirm this? And since the government of the state must everywhere be equal according to its degrees, so the condition of the power of the state must to some extent be in agreement with that of the nobility in their households, as may be sufficiently shown by other regions.

To the second). As far as favourites are concerned, it is true that the state sometimes suffers many misfortunes from them. This indeed happened more in republics, as we read in ancient Greek and Roman history, how having strengthened themselves certain magnates brought about great ruin by internecine war. And this must be particularly feared by us, and examples need hardly be searched for in monarchies, I do not want to look far, but we all know enough how violent favourites brought about complete ruin; Skuratov and Basmonov – tsar Ivan

Vasil'evich, Miloslavskii — tsar Fedor Alekseevich; Menshikov, Tolstoi and others in our own time. On the other hand, there are the wise and faithful; Mstislavskii, Romanov, Shuiskii — tsar Ivan; Boris Morozov and Streshnev — tsar Aleksei; Bogdan Khitroi and Iazikov — tsar Fedor Alekseevich; Prince Vasilii Golitsyn — the tsarevna Sof'ia — they earned great honour and gratitude for ever, although some through hate of others finished their lives in misfortune.

To the third). Although very old and in existence if not under Augustus, then under Tiberius his successor, the secret chancellery was devised for the security of the monarch, and it is in no way harmful if entrusted to an honourable man. Bad and dishonourable men do not enjoy the position for long but disappear, as we see with all historical and recent examples. Leaving all the foregoing, we must now look at the present.

On the sovereign empress, although we are sufficiently convinced of her wisdom, virtue and orderly government in Courland, however, she is a female person and this is inconvenient for many difficulties; the more so in that her knowledge of the laws is inadequate. And so for a time, until the Almighty gives us a male person on the throne, it is necessary to arrange something for the help of Her Highness. After discussing it enough for three days, we put forward the following suggestions:

(1)   let there be with Her Majesty in the higher government, the senate, twenty-one persons, in which the present Supreme Council will remain.

(2)   In order that it will not be burdened by affairs of the internal economy, let another government be set up of one hundred persons, of which a third will be in government for each third of the year, and two thirds may carry on their own household affairs. But at the end of each third, that is in December, April, August, or at the beginning — January, May and September, for the consideration of important affairs they should assemble each year. Or when something unusual occurs, such as war, the death of a sovereign, or another such important event, then summon all together, and the general assembly should continue for no more than a month.

(3)   If there is a vacancy in the higher assembly, the senate, college, president and vice-president, in the provinces, governor or deputy governor, in the armed forces, commander in chief, then the presidents of the colleges should be elected by the ballot of the two houses of government; and a commander in the forces, unlike the presidents, by all military generals, together with those houses of government. The ballot should be carried out on the following manner; the heraldmaster must read the list of all those

worthy to be candidates in order of rank; then each elector must write on a paper the name of him whom he considers to be worthy, and put it completed in a box. Having scrutinised the papers in the presence of all, the heraldmaster is to write on a list, which name received how many votes, and which received more votes, and of them three are to be ballotted, and he who receives most balls of approval is to be presented to Her Highness, and if ballot by balls is not suitable, then it is enough to determine whom of the three who received most votes should be presented to Her Highness. In this manner there may be worthy people in the whole of government, irrespective of high birth, through which many unsuitable people are promoted.

(4)   Although promulgation of laws is solely in the power of the monarch, as pointed out above, however on reflection the purpose of the sovereign is nothing else than the general good and justice, as it must be exactly observed. And as it does not please Her Majesty to draft laws herself, but is necessary for somebody to be entrusted with the draft, there is no small danger that somebody might through caprice bring in something improper and unjust or even harmful. Therefore, Peter the Great, although he was a wise sovereign, saw much in his own laws that needed to be changed, for which he ordered all of them to be collected, examined and drafted anew. And so, it is better to examine before promulgation than to change afterwards that which is not consonant with the honour of the monarch. This drafting must not in any be entrusted to one person who, although he is skilful and has none of his own bias in his intention, might naturally err. And so as soon as a law is drawn up at the command of Her Majesty, let it be sent to all the colleges, so that they might examine it sufficiently, and after seven days each of them generally or individually should in assembly inform the higher government, and drafting it after sufficient discussion present it to Her Highness for confirmation.

(5)   It is very improper when in one department of government there is a father with a son, or two brothers, or an uncle with a nephew, father-in-law with son-in-law, who would have two votes conferred on them. And so there should not be two of one family in the higher government. And in the lower and in the colleges there should not be close relatives as shown above.

(6)   Although in the Secret Chancellery there should be somebody assigned by Her Majesty, there should also be assigned from the senate two persons every month, to see justice done. And one distinguished man from the police should always be taken on so that there is no less concern during confiscation of property.

(7)   For the promotion of the nobility in the armed forces and the

civil service there should be a better method than now. (1) The necessary schools should be built in all towns, and funds and buildings should be assigned to them. (2) Service should not be obligatory for those less than eighteen years of age, or last for more than twenty years in the forces. (3) There should be no enrolment as sailors or tradesmen. (4) So that the genuine nobility should be known, a register should be made in the whole state, not including those who are from the soldiers, hussars, small-holders *[odnodvortsy]* and petty officials *[pod'iachie]* , although they possess many villages, unless thay have charters granted to estates or nobility. However all those of whatever rank who already have villages should be written in a separate book.

(8) The income of the priesthood should be examined so that the rural clergy might keep their children in schools and not have to plough themselves; and whoever has surpluses, let them be used for purposes beneficial to God and the state.

(9) Merchants should be freed as much as possible from billeting and restrictions, and given the capability of increasing manufacture and trade.

(10) The points about inheritance [the *maiorat* of 1714] should be abolished, and an adequate law on the basis of the Code [of 1649] should be drawn up.

Presenting this to the Supreme Council, we demand that they should order all the nobility to elect for the examination of this [dissertation] worthy people, not less than one hundred people.

[There follow details of procedure to be adopted concerning the Dissertation and the signatures appended to it.]

From *Utro, literaturnyi sbornik*, M., 1859.

3. The Manifesto on the Freedom of the Nobility, 1762

INTRODUCTION

Once the autocracy of Anna was assured, she did away with the Supreme Privy Council. The Dolgorukiis were sent into exile, and D.M. Golitsyn, although made a senator, virtually retired to his estate. A new establishment was created of mixed Russian and German complexion, and with a change of patrons came the fresh clamour of clients. A Scottish mercenary officer, James Keith, who was surprised at the time to be promoted to Lieutenant-Colonel in the Guards, soon discovered that "as the emploiement is looked on as one of the greatest trusts in the Empire, and that the officers of the Guards are regarded as domesticks of the Souveraign, I received hundreds of visits from people I had never seen nor heard of in my life . . ."[1] Keith was not alone in his rapid elevation, which occurred particularly in the Guards but was also to be found in other branches of service, and such jumps past several rungs of the rank ladder were numerous not only at the accession of Anna but at that of her successors, too. For example, in an energetic attempt to shore up her Regency at the death of the Empress Anna in 1740, another Anna — Leopol'dovna pushed several higher members of the bureaucracy past two or even three rungs. As a rationale for such speedy advancement, recognition was given in several decrees of the period of "distinguished services" *[zaslugi]* as opposed to "seniority" *[vysluga]* .

At the same time as the series of "palace revolutions" from 1725 to 1762, there was an underlying tendency towards the regularisation of promotion in the armed forces and especially in the bureaucracy. The daughter of Peter the Great, the Empress Elizabeth, duly elevated her own men after over-throwing the Regency of Anna Leopol'dovna in 1740. However, her government addressed itself later in decrees of 1753 and 1754 to arranging procedures of advancement with the cooperation of the functionaries themselves, who were collectively to work out their own exact positions in the hierarchy. Troitskii tells us:

"With these measures the government of Elizaveta Petrovna tried to put order into the advancement of functionaries according to the principle of personal seniority. All other criteria had a subordinate significance. In fact, as has been properly noted in the literature, the instructions of the government, beginning with the General Regulations of the colleges and the Table of Ranks and finishing with the decrees of

28

1753-4 introduced instead of a system of preference by pedigree such a system by office and rank. Such a practice, in the opinion of the government, must stimulate the service fervour of the functionaries."[2]

This regularisation of promotion tended to reinforce two tendencies: the bureaucratisation of the nobility; and the ennoblement of bureaucrats. Many members of the ruling class were not happy with either tendency, particularly the second, and the government made a positive response to their discontent. Decrees of 1755, 1758 and 1760 reiterated earlier governmental attempts to keep commoners out of the dvorianstvo. Special attention had previously been paid to local government. This was partly because Peter the Great's schemes for reform in this sphere had been far too elaborate; and so, in the years immediately following his death, 1726-7, municipal and provincial offices predominated in a reduction by twenty-seven of the number of ranks in the Table. And then, decrees of 1737, 1739 and 1742 attempted to inhibit local administrators from advancing commoners in their service to noble rank.

The necessity for governments to repeat their attempts to restrict the ennoblement of commoner functionaries had been brought about largely by the reluctance and incompetence of the dvorianstvo to fill the administrative offices by itself. Indeed, governments were more than once forced to admit that there was an insufficiency of capable dvoriane and that recourse would have to be made to commoners. Peter the Great had attempted to ensure that there would be enough young nobles in the civil branch of the service by giving such junkers special incentives and advantages and by punishing those who concealed themselves or absconded from service – the *netchiki*. Even he had been obliged to confess at least partial defeat, and his successors found themselves caught in the same dilemma. How could the bureaucracy be adequate for the state's increasing needs without reducing the influence in it of the dvorianstvo?

This question was one of the principal subjects for discussions connected with the Legislative Commission convened towards the end of the reign of the Empress Elizabeth. Two distinct views appear to have been put forward concerning the leading part generally to be played in the Russian Empire by its ruling class. On the one hand, the brothers M.I. and R.I. Vorontsov were anxious to increase the privileges of the nobility in such a manner that something like a true aristocracy would be created. They welcomed the advancement of noble courtiers and diplomats which had occurred during Elizabeth's reign, and wanted to extend their economic privileges, too, in such a manner that something like an English aristocracy would be created. For this purpose, it would be necessary to emancipate the nobility from service. On the other hand, the brothers P.I. and A.I. Shuvalov were opposed to a

29

general emancipation, preferring a division of the nobility into a service corps and an "embourgeoisified" group of entrepreneurs. The debate was resolved after the death of Elizabeth and the accession of her nephew, Peter III, in the Manifesto on the Freedom of the Nobility of 18 February 1762. The Vorontsovs realised their ambitions for an emancipation, but strings were attached and no mention made of privileges in agriculture, trade or industry.

In this brief introduction, we obviously cannot embark on a full consideration of Peter III's somewhat enigmatic reign, but must rather concentrate on placing the Manifesto in a general and then in a specific context. Firstly, many if by no means all observers have seen it as a culmination of an irregular but persistent progress away from the obligations and rigours of service imposed on the nobility by Peter the Great. According to this interpretation, the dvorianstvo's antipathy to conscription, already apparent during Peter's lifetime, was made completely clear in the projects composed at the time of the succession crisis of 1730. Explicit demands were put forward for curtailment of the length of service to 20-25 years, commencement of service with advantages and continuance of it with regular and adequate pay. The nobles also asked in 1730 for exclusive educational institutions and for the abolition of the hated decree of Peter the Great of 1714 which prescribed single inheritance of property rather than the partitional division among all surviving children. Anna's government acceded to these demands with a series of decrees throughout her reign, and her successors were scarcely less obliging. Although conditions of service were now far less rigorous, nobles continued to hide away from it, and occasionally the government felt constrained to apply pressure and even punishment. A decree of 1749 ordered retired dvoriane to register with the Heralds and present themselves to the senate for assignment to further service. During the years 1743-1750, 801 out of 8753 young noblemen (i.e. 9.1%) registered for service deserted before receiving assignments. Most of these were condemned to permanent reduction to the ranks, some to enrolment as ordinary seamen, and a few to exile to Orenburg. All except 92 were in fact pardoned after the intercession of the senate. Then, during the Seven Years War, conscription was necessarily fairly strict. Nevertheless, the period from 1725 to 1762 can still be called one of irregular progress towards emancipation, and the Manifesto, therefore, be seen as its culmination. Accompanying the gradual transformation of service from an obligation to a privilege were such tendencies as the replacement of land as a reward by pay in the general context of a burgeoning money economy: the development of provincial life in which noble landlords would be predominant; and the growth of the self-consciousness and self-confidence of the dvorianstvo during the series of palace revolutions.

A stimulating antithesis to the traditional interpretation of the Manifesto was put forward by Marc Raeff in 1966:

"Far from marking the nobility's 'victory' over the state, as frequently stated, the decree of 1762 marked rather the state's declaration of 'independence' from the services of the nobility. That is why even though it secured permission to remain idle, the status and rights of the nobility witnessed no change or expansion. Whatever rights the nobility would obtain subsequently were to give further expression to the state's independence from its services. Thus the government attempted to direct the nobleman's energies into new channels outside of state service and make them more useful to both country and people by having them involve themselves more in their private affairs as landowners. No longer did the state need the nobleman for service, but it still wanted him to help westernise and modernise the country, to be a social and cultural leader of the people."[3]

Raeff reiterated his view of the emancipation of the Russian nobility, albeit with some modification, in 1970, and Robert E. Jones followed Raeff in an eponymous monograph on the subject in 1973. Historical revisions are always welcome, and undoubtedly the emancipation must be seen in the context of the arguments about the part that the dvorianstvo should play in the Russian Empire put forward by the Vorontsovs, Shuvalovs and others in the 1750s and 1760s. The greatest weakness of the Raeff-Jones interpretation appears to be a tendency towards reification of the state and oversimplification of the social structure of the dvorianstvo. The Vorontsovs, Shuvalovs and their like were not separate from the state, but constituted an important part of it. Lower-ranking dvoriane were not divided from such grandees by an impenetrable gulf, but rather inextricably bound to them by networks of patronage, in which the client of today could be the patron of tomorrow.

But such a summary exposition does full justice to neither view of the Manifesto and its significance. Readers are therefore urged not only to examine the following translation but also to acquaint themselves with the relevant analytical literature. Let us leave the last word here with Kliuchevskii, who wrote: "The law said: be so good, serve and teach your children, and nevertheless he who does neither the one nor the other will be driven from society."[4]

Footnotes
1. Field-Marshal James Keith, *A Fragment of a Memoir of . . . written by himself, 1714-1734,* Edinburgh 1843, p.90.
2. S.M. Troitskii, *Russkii absoliutizm,* p.130.
3. M. Raeff, *Origins,* p.109.
4. Quoted by P. Dukes, *Catherine the Great,* p.43n.

Manifesto on the Freedom of the Nobility
Complete Collection of the Laws of the Russian Empire, First Series, 1649-1825, Volume 15, pp.912-15, No. 11,444, 18 February 1762

Our grandfather Peter the Great, Emperor of all the Russias, of undying fame, most wise monarch and gracious sovereign, was obliged to bear such a burden and so many difficulties solely for the happiness and advantage of his fatherland while raising up Russia to the complete knowledge of military, civil and political affairs, of which not only Europe but also the large part of the world is the true witness.

For this revival it was first of all necessary to show the noble dvorianstvo as chief member of the state how great were the advantages of enlightened powers in human prosperity compared with the numberless peoples sunk in the depths of ignorance; but at that time extreme need made it necessary that he should order the Russian dvorianstvo to show its recognition for the kindness done to it by entering military and civil service. Moreover, the noble youth had to study useful arts and sciences; they were sent to European states and various schools were set up in Russia so that the desired fruits should be achieved with the greatest speed.

It is true that such arrangements turned out to be burdensome and unbearable for the nobility at the beginning depriving them of their peace, taking them away from home, making them carry out military and other services against their will and enrolling their children in them, from which some hid themselves away and were thus subjected not only to fines but even to the loss of their estates for being negligent of their own good and of that of their descendants.

All who occupied the Russian throne from the times of Peter the Great continued the arrangement referred to above, which was very useful although attended with compulsion at the beginning. Our gracious aunt particularly, the Sovereign Empress Elizabeth Petrovna of blessed memory, imitated the deeds of her sovereign father by spreading and increasing knowledge of political affairs and various sciences under her patronage in the Russian state. We see with pleasure what arose from all this, and each true son of the fatherland must recognise that countless benefits have followed from it: coarseness in those who neglect the general good has been eradicated, ignorance has been transformed into healthy reason, useful knowledge and assiduity in service have increased the number of skilful and brave generals in military affairs, have put informed and suitable people in civil and political affairs, to conclude in a word, noble thoughts have implanted in the hearts of all true Russian patriots a boundless loyalty and love for Us, a great enthusiasm and unceasing fervency for our service, and therefore We do not find that necessity for compulsion in service, which was in effect up to this time.

And so, in the light of those circumstances referred to, by the authority vested in Us by the Most High, by Our Highest Imperial Grace, We now and henceforth for all time and for all generations to come bestow on the whole Russian noble dvorianstvo freedom and liberty, and they may continue service both in Our Empire and in other European states allied to Us, on the basis of the following enactments:

1. All the dvoriane in the various branches of Our service may continue in it for as long as they wish and their circumstances permit. However those in military service may not ask for leave or emancipation from service in times of campaigns or for three months before them, but at their conclusion both inside and outside the state, they may ask their commanders for emancipation from service or retirement and await the decision: those in the top eight ranks of the various branches of Our service — with Our supreme confirmation, and other ranks — by the decision of the departments to which they belong.

2. All serving dvoriane should be rewarded on retirement for honest and blameless service by one rank if they have been for more than a year in the former rank with which they go into retirement, and the same should apply to those who ask for emancipation from all affairs. Those who want to leave military for civil service when there are vacancies should be appointed according to an examination and be rewarded if they have been three years in one rank, that is in that with which they go into civil or other service.

3. Whoever has been in retirement for some time or is in civil and other service after military service and now wants to enter military service will be accepted if he turns out to be worthy of it with the rank he presently holds transferred into a military rank, but with seniority lower than those in the rank with whom he was emancipated from military service. If he has already been promoted, the man being assigned to military service will receive seniority from the day on which he is assigned. And We decree that those serving should have advantage and preference before those not serving. In like manner, whoever has retired from civil service and later wants to enter civil and other service apart from the military, will be accepted according to his suitability, according to this same clause except for the manner of the transfer alone.

4. Whoever has been freed from Our service and wants to go to other European states should be given the appropriate passports of Our College of Foreign Affairs, with the condition that when necessity demands, the dvoriane who are outside the state should make their appearance in the fatherland. As soon as the necessary announcement is

made about this, then everybody in such a situation must carry out Our wishes with all possible speed under pain of sequestration of his estate.

5. The Russian dvoriane who are engaged in service with other European sovereigns may return to the fatherland and enter Our service according to their wishes and the existing vacancies: those in the service of crowned heads with the ranks for which they show patents, and those with other masters — with a lowering of rank, as established by former legislation and as will be carried out now.

6. And as by this Our gracious decree none of the Russian dvoriane will continue service against his will, they will not be used in national affairs by Our instituted government, unless particular necessity demands and then not otherwise than with a personal decree signed by Our own hand, the same with the Smolensk nobility. However, it was ordered by the decree of Peter the First that in Moscow and St. Petersburg in the senate and its office there should be several of the retired dvoriane for all requirements occurring there. And so We royally command that henceforth every year in rotation there should be up to thirty men in the senate and twenty men in its office, for which the Heralds should arrange a detail annually of those living in the provinces and those not in service. However they should not assign anybody by name, but the dvoriane in the provinces and counties should carry on elections among themselves and report to the local chancelleries, which will in turn report to the Heralds and arrange for the transfer of those elected.

7. Although by this Our gracious enactment all the Russian dvoriane excluding the smallholders will always be able to have their freedom, Our paternal concern for them stretches even further to their young children, whom henceforth solely for information We order to appear before the Heralds at the age of twelve in the provinces, counties and towns, wherever is more convenient and suitable, and their parents or the relations with whom they are at the inspection should say what they have learned before the age of twelve and where they want to continue their education further, inside Our state at the various institutions kept up at Our expense, or in other European countries, or at home with clever and learned teachers if their parents have enough property to allow this to be done. However, so that nobody should dare to bring up his children without teaching them the subjects fitting for the noble dvorianstvo under pain of our wrath, for this we order all those dvoriane who have not more than a thousand peasants to report their children directly to Our Noble Military Academy, where they will be educated with the most enthusiastic care and each will leave with a reward of ranks appropriate to his educational achievement and later enter and continue service according to the above prescription.

8. Those dvoriane who are now in service as soldiers and other ranks

below commissioned officer should not be retired unless they have done more than twelve years service.

9. But as we enact this Our most gracious arrangement for the whole noble dvorianstvo as a fundamental and unbroken law for all time, in conclusion with Our Imperial word in a most solemn manner We confirm it forever to be kept sacrosanct and uninfringed with all the stated force and advantages. Our lawful descendants could do anything to abolish it, but the preservation of this enactment will be for them an unshakable confirmation of the autocratic throne. On the other hand, We hope that the whole noble dvorianstvo, appreciative of our generosity to them and their descendants, will be inspired by their most dutiful loyalty to Us and their zeal, not to absent or hide themselves from service, but to enter it with pride and enthusiasm, and continue it in an honourable and decent manner to the extent of their ability, and none the less teaching their children suitable subjects with diligence and application, because all those who have not been in service anywhere, but spend all their time in sloth and idleness, and do not subject their children to any useful education for the benefit of the fatherland, these as they are negligent of the common good, We command all Our obedient and true sons to despise and scorn, and they will not be allowed to appear at Our Court, or at public meetings and celebrations.

4. Catherine II's Directions to Prince A.A. Viazemskii on his Assumption of the Position of Procurator-General, 1764

INTRODUCTION

The impact of the Manifesto of 1762 would depend largely on the attitude to it of Catherine II, who seized the throne in June of that year after her husband's forceful removal from it. The Manifesto itself had said that, while freedom from service would be introduced "for all the noble dvorianstvo for all time as a fundamental and certain rule", its preservation would require the "unshakable affirmation" of the Emperor's lawful successors. The usurper Catherine, who proclaimed herself to be the first of these, noted early on in her reign to Nikita Panin, one of her chief advisers, that there was considerable murmuring among the nobility about the non-confirmation of its freedom, and set up a special committee or commission at the beginning of 1763 expressly to consider that question. The commission's deliberations appear to have discussed freedom from service less than advantages to be gained in service. It also stressed the importance of restricting the entry into the dvorianstvo of commoners and of giving top members of the class advantages over their lesser brethren. Catherine shelved the commission's recommendations, but at least two decrees of 1766 and another of 1768 confirmed the Manifesto of 1762, and there was no suggestion that Catherine's government would revert to the peremptory policies of Peter the Great.

After her accession, Catherine attempted to shore up her somewhat unstable position by sharing out the spoils of imperial patronage among her entourage, which in turn rewarded its own adherents. In such a manner, the new establishment managed to install itself without serious opposition. Closest to the Empress at first were Gregory Orlov, her current lover, and his brothers and associates in the all-important Guards, while the most significant figure on the civil side was Nikita I. Panin, tutor to her son Paul. While there may have been no serious threat to this new group at the apex of power, there was much rumour of plot and counterplot among disgruntled rivals, and at least one or two actual conspiracies. Later analysis has extended suspicion as far as Panin himself, who was jockeying for position with the Orlovs and putting forward the view that his royal pupil had a more legitimate claim to the throne than that young man's mother. More than one historian has descried an attempt at oligarchic takeover in the project for an Imperial Council that Panin composed at Catherine's invitation.

However, not only would such a challenge have been out of character, there is also no concrete evidence for it; indeed, when the Council was actually created in 1768, a British diplomat observed that Panin, a man of "circumspection and cautiousness",[1] was in favour of it because it would forestall any attempt at oligarchy by the brothers Zakhar and Peter Chernyshev.

Back in 1762, Panin was aiming mostly at administrative efficiency, partly through the introduction of the Council, partly through the division of the senate into six different departments. As David Ransel says:

> "The two sections of the reform project were integrally related. The effectiveness of one section depended on the implementation of the other. The institution of the one or the other separately would undermine the whole scheme. To divide the senate into departments, and increase the number of senators without at the same time creating the Imperial Council would simply weaken the senate diminishing its ability to guard the interests of the established families against the depredations of court favourites. By the same token, to create the Imperial Council without reducing the senate and circumscribing its activities would amount to placing two high government bodies with similar functions in competition with one another. This arrangement would do little to improve the efficiency of government. It was this integral relation between the two parts of the reform that prompted Panin to press for the establishment of the whole project immediately, before other persons could have time 'to shape it the way they themselves would wish' ".[2]

Panin was perhaps remembering that Peter III was probably brought down at least partly by the failure of himself and his closest associates to manage the higher administration in a balanced manner. As for Catherine, she moved somewhat circumspectly towards the creation of the Council, although it did previously enjoy a *de facto* existence in the shape of the committee on the nobility, whose personnel was identical to that of the Council when it was finally set up in 1768.

The senate reform came in more quickly on 15 December 1763. The first and foremost of the six new divisions was to deal with a wide range of important economic and political affairs, and the Procurator-General was to be at its head. The other five departments were to concern themselves respectively with: petitions and appeals; the Ukraine, Finland and Baltic Provinces, higher academic affairs, ports, communications and police; army and navy, young noble academies, the Smolensk nobility, customs posts and New Serbia; state business in Moscow; and appeals against the second department. On the same day, further decrees attempted to put some order into provincial government through improvement in the pay and regulation in the sphere of duty of its officials, as well as through the considerable increase of their number. In 1764 came a more general reorganisation of the Table of Ranks, the biggest since the 1720s. Academicians and state factory managers were brought into the Table as other positions were adjusted in central and local government and police, and the Heraldmaster was promoted to rank 5.

At the beginning of her reign, like her predecessors, Catherine had favoured "distinguished services" over "seniority" as a basis for promotion. Senators and others had protested about this, and there was considerable unease among bureaucrats about the widening gap between rank and office. Once her new men were firmly in position, Catherine responded to this dissatisfaction in 1767 and brought in regular septennial promotion. For the rest of the reign, Catherine was never happy with the way in which her administration functioned, although the senate and Council achieved a comfortable enough coexistence, and she contemplated further reforms of the central government in 1788 and 1794. But action came in the provincial sphere, where the decrees of 1775 brought in sweeping changes, extending as far as the central Colleges, which we will be examining below. The 1775 reform made the Procurator-General even more important than he was before; now he was like a minister with three ministries — finance, internal affairs and justice.

It is high time we took a look at the man chosen by Catherine to fill this important office. Prince Alexander Alekseevich Viazemskii was born in 1727, and educated at the Serpukhov noble academy. He was already rising quickly in service when Catherine chose him in 1763 to go to the mines and works of the Urals to settle a revolt and to find out about their economic performance. He was chosen next year to be Procurator-General in place of A.I. Glebov who had been found guilty of financial malpractice. He gained the trust of the Empress through diligent execution of the directions that she gave him on the assumption of the office, and his duties grew along with her confidence. He achieved a reputation for discretion as well as conscientiousness, and was able to stay aloof from the intrigues of the court and the machinations of politics. The two parties referred to below in direction 3 are in turn the Orlovs and Panins. At that time, Catherine favoured the Orlovs, but not without reservation. Their patron earlier on had been Peter Shuvalov, of whom the Empress had emphatically expressed her disapproval in section 1, and she could never escape the feeling that those whom she had promoted above all others would try to dominate her. So the Panins were never ousted by the Orlovs and were sometimes in the ascendancy over them. And then in 1774, a new favourite Gregory Potemkin came to the fore; still, although the institutions of the government had been made much more elaborate, the power over it of persons was not diminished to any great degree. And so a man whom Catherine could trust, the inclinations of her heart apart, and the squabbling of factions above, was worth a great amount to her. Hence the importance of Viazemskii, who retained the confidence of Catherine beyond lovers and politicians until a stroke in 1789 led to retirement in 1792, four years before his own death and that of the Empress.

Footnotes

1. W. Shirley, *Egerton Ms. 2699*, ff.285-6. British Museum.
2. D. Ransel, *The Politics*, pp.93-4.

Catherine II's Directions to Prince A.A. Viazemskii on his Assumption of the Position of Procurator-General

Most secret directions to Prince Viazemskii. You already know that you will be taking up the position of procurator-general.

1) The former bad conduct, self-interest, extortion and bad reputation as a consequence of these characteristics, the insufficient candour and sincerity towards Me of the present procurator-general, – all this forces Me to replace him, and completely obscures and destroys his ability and diligence in affairs; and it must be added that no small contribution to his misfortune was his acquaintance and close relations while still in his youth with the late Count Peter Shuvalov, in whose hands he was completely, and whose principles he drank in, although they were not very useful for society, but profitable enough for themselves. All this brought about his inclination to shady rather than to straightforward affairs, and his frequent concealment from Me of much of his behaviour, as a result of which My confidence in him diminished proportionately; and nothing can be more harmful for society, than such a procurator-general, who does not have complete candour and openness towards the Sovereign, since he is bound to be in opposition to the most powerful people in his position, and consequently the power of the the Sovereign is his sole support.

2) You must know with whom you are dealing. Everyday incidents will lead you to Me. You will find in Me that I have no other views, than the greatest happiness and glory of the fatherland, and I desire nothing so much as the prosperity of My subjects whatever rank they are.

My thoughts aspire only to the preservation of quietness, contentment and calm inside and outside the State. If I see in you loyalty, diligence and open candour, you may flatter yourself that you will receive from Me boundless confidence. I very much love the truth, and you may speak it completely without fear and argue with me without danger, so long only as affairs go well. I hear that you are considered to be an honourable man; I hope to show you through experience that at court people with these qualities live happily. And I add to that, that I do not demand flattery from you, but only sincere conduct and steadfastness in affairs.

3) In the senate you will find two parties, but a sensible policy on My part demands that they should not be respected, so that they should not be allowed to solidify and will disappear all the more quickly, and I have kept watch on them with a vigilant eye, and have used people according to their capabilities for this and that task. Both parties will now try to lure you over to their side. You will find in one

people of good morals, although sometimes not of perspicacious intellects, in the other, I think, their views extend further, but it is not clear if they are always useful. Somebody thinks that because he has been for a long time in this or that land, that everything everywhere must be arranged according to the policy in his favourite land, and everything else without exception earns his criticism, in spite of the fact that everywhere internal arrangements are based on the disposition of the people. You must not respect either one or the other side, but must treat each courteously and impartially, and listen to each, having in view only the benefit of the fatherland and justice and progress with firm steps by the shortest route to the truth. Ask Me about anything of which you are doubtful and trust completely in God and Me, and I, seeing your conduct pleasing to Me will not abandon you. You will deserve through the principles written above respect from various people, you will be a terror to the idle and a protection for honourable people.

4) All offices and the senate itself have come away from their foundations for various reasons, such as the lack of application to affairs of certain of My predecessors, and the predilections of their more unofficial people. The senate was set up for the execution of the laws assigned to it, and it often issued laws and distributed ranks, honours, money, villages, in a word almost everything, and restricted other judicial offices in their laws and advantages. So that I happened to hear in the senate, that they wanted to reprimand one of the colleges for nothing more than daring to present its opinions to the senate. This however I did not allow, but told the gentlemen present that they should be pleased to see the law carried out. Through such persecution of the lower offices they had gone into such a decline that they had completely forgotten the Regulations, according to which it was ordered that representations should be made to the senate and consequently to Me about senate decrees which were not valid in law. The servility of people in these offices is indescribable, and no good can be expected until this evil is eradicated. One bureaucratic procedure only is carried out, and they just do not dare to think of others, although the state interest suffers. The senate having alone transgressed its boundaries is now with difficulty accustomed to the order in which it must be. Possibly, former examples are attractive to certain members for their ambition; however, while I live, we will remain as duty commands. The Russian Empire is so large, that apart from the Autocratic Sovereign every other form of government is harmful to it, because all others are slower in their execution and contain a great multitude of various horrors, which lead to the disintegration of power and strength more than that of one Sovereign, who possesses all the means for the eradication of all harm and looks on the general good as

his own, and others are all, in the words of the Gospel, hirelings.

5) Because of the size of the Empire there is a great need for an increase in the circulation of money. We have now according to the calculations of the Money Department not more than eighty millions of silver among the people, which sum distributed according to the number of people comes to four roubles a head, if not less. There have been various projects, of which there has finally been copper coin, about which there has been very many complaints; however until there is an outstanding increase of silver in the state, this evil must be borne, and there must now be the attempt, as has already been worked out, to stop various weights of coin constituting the same value and various values of one weight of metal, so that silver may be attracted into the state by all possible means, such as for example by the grain trade, as the trade commission has already ordered. About the issue of silver I cannot say anything else than that this matter is very delicate, and it is unpleasant to many to hear about it, however you must try to understand this matter as well. I write all this to introduce you to these most secret matters so that you will not be new to them when you take up affairs and may choose yourself which are actually useful, or only seem to be.

6) It will be most difficult of all for you to govern the Senate Chancellery, and not to be deceived by subordinates. I represent this particular to you more clearly through an example. The French Cardinal De Richelieu, this most wise minister, said that there was less difficulty for him to govern the state and arrange Europe according to his intentions than to rule the King's Antechamber, because all the idle courtiers were against him and hindered his great intentions with their base intrigues. One means only remains to you, which Richelieu did not have, to replace all the doubtful and suspicious without mercy.

7) Our laws demand correction, firstly, so that all might be arranged in one system which is to be maintained; secondly, so that those which contradict it are got rid of; thirdly, to separate the temporary and the personal from the permanent and the indispensable, about which there has already been thought, but shortness of time has not yet allowed Me to put it into effect.

8) It is a great burden for the people to have salt and liquor on the same basis as they are now, there are so many guilty of bootlegging that it is almost impossible to punish them, since whole counties are subject to it; and since it is impossible to eradicate, it is not bad to seek means of correction and the relief of the people.

9) Little Russia, Livonia and Finland are provinces, which are governed by confirmed privileges. To destroy them by the suspension of them all immediately would be very unseemly; however to call them foreign and to deal with them on such a basis is more than a mistake,

and may truly be called stupidity. These provinces, as well as Smolensk, must by the easiest of means be brought to the point where they would russify and cease to look like wolves to the forest; this will be a very easy step, if reasonable people are chosen as commanders in these provinces; when there is no Hetman in Little Russia, then there must be an attempt to make disappear the era and name of the Hetman, not just the promotion of some person into that distinction.

From N.D. Chechulin and others, eds., *Istoriia pravitel'stvuiushchego senata za dvesti let, 1711-1911*, vol. 2, SPB, 1911, rep. ORP, 1973, Appendix XVI.

5. S.E. Desnitskii's Proposal for the Establishment of Legislative, Judicial and Executive Power in the Russian Empire, 1768

INTRODUCTION

During the first years of her reign, Catherine applied herself to the theoretical as well as the practical aspects of her administration. Apart from reforming the senate and other central and provincial institutions, she worked very hard on her *Nakaz* or her Instructions to the Legislative Commission of 1767. This document incorporated many of the ideas of Montesquieu and Beccaria, and some of those of the cameralists, encyclopedists and physiocrats, to such an extent that Catherine could write to Frederick II of Prussia without false modesty: "I have acted like the crow of the fable who made itself a garment of peacock's feathers".[1] Catherine made skilful use of these and other sources to provide a rationale for her own absolutism, which, she asserted, was more consonant with the size and nature of the Russian Empire than any other form of government. In a Supplement to the *Nakaz* on the State Economy in 1768, Catherine adopted some of the ideas of Adam Smith relayed to her by S.E. Desnitskii, who had put them in his "Proposal for the Establishment of Legislative, Judicial and Executive Power in the Russian Empire".

Semen Efimovich Desnitskii was born in the town of Nezhin in the Ukraine, the son of a petty burgher. The exact date of his birth is unknown, but it was probably either at the end of the 1730s or the beginning of the 1740s. After some years at the seminary attached to the Troitsko-Sergeivskoi Monastery, he transferred to the gymnasium attached to Moscow University. In 1759 he entered the University itself, but was soon sent on to the Academy of Sciences in St. Petersburg, where he studied physics, philosophy, and *elokventsiia* or rhetoric. In 1761 he was ordered to go to Glasgow University along with I.A. Tret'iakov, and the two young Russians stayed in Scotland until 1767.

As A.H. Brown points out, the Scottish Enlightenment was by no means the exclusive affair of Edinburgh. During the years that Desnitskii and his companion were in Glasgow, not only Adam Smith and John Millar were on the staff of the University, but also Thomas Reid, the Common-Sense philosopher who transferred from Aberdeen to succeed Smith in 1764; Joseph Black, Professor of Medicine and lecturer in Chemistry until 1766, a brilliant scientific innovator; and James Watt, who was mathematical instrument-maker to the University. At the same time as experiencing considerable financial and personal difficulties, the Russian pair were able to absorb a great amount of the new, as well as of the old, learning.

On their return to Moscow as Doctors of Law, they found their Scottish qualifications unacceptable to the German-dominated University, and had to undergo further examinations. They both did well in law, Desnitskii particularly, and were given teaching positions. Desnitskii went on to a distinguished career, becoming a founder member of the Russian Academy in 1783, and making major contributions to that Academy's dictionary, particularly its legal and political terms. He retired from Moscow University in 1787 and died in 1789.

Brown tells us that the greatest influences on Desnitskii were Smith and Millar; Lomonosov, Montesquieu and Blackstone (part of whose work he translated) were also of some significance in this respect. Desnitskii paid his Scottish mentors a great compliment by quoting from them at great length, although the borrowing would have been more gracious if it had been acknowledged. At the same time, Desnitskii was much more than an enthusiastic plagiarist, demonstrating a considerable independence of thought in his work on political and social institutions, comparative law and, in his first publications, on economic policy. Soviet analysts have exaggerated the originality of his comparative-historical approach and specifically his exposition of four stages in the development of society: 1) hunting; 2) pastoral; 3) agricultural; 4) commercial. Yet he at least partly reworked them in his own way, and their early appearance in Russia in any form is of no small significance.

A.H. Brown considers that the Proposal in particular puts forward many "acute observations and interesting proposals for reform". He continues:

"In summary, it is fair to say that its implementation would have set Russia far along the path towards constitutional monarchy. Desntisky is an opponent of arbitrary power in all its forms, whether that of a provincial governor, of a landowner, or (though here he has to be more guarded) of an autocrat. Though it goes without saying that he cannot attack the absolute power of the monarch directly, Desnitsky's desire to create strong political institutions and his advocacy of a separation of the legislative, judicial, executive, and civic authorities, so that one would act as an overseer and check upon another, would lead not only to a curb upon the power of the nobility and (especially given the social composition proposed by Desnitsky for the legislature and civic authorities) an increase in the power of commercial and professional interests. It would also have its effect upon the autocracy. The establishment of a representative assembly, of an independent judiciary, and of an executive authority subordinate to the law could scarcely, except in the very short term, be compatible with a continuation of the absolute power of the monarch. Given Desnitsky's close familiarity with, and admiration for, the British constitutional model, it is more than likely that he anticipated just such a gradual development towards constitutional monarchy."[2]

In such circumstances, it is not surprising that, although presented to Catherine II in early 1768, the *Proposal* was not published until 1905, an appropriate enough year, for it was then that at last the Russian autocracy began to take the direction that Desnitskii had set out for it nearly a century and a half before.

Footnotes

1. Quoted by P. Dukes, *Catherine the Great*, p.56.
2. A.H. Brown, "S.E. Desnitsky", p.49.

Proposal for the Establishment of Legislative, Judicial and Executive Power in the Russian Empire.

Most Gracious Sovereign!

Loyalty and zeal, such fitting offerings to sovereigns from subjects, can be rendered to none of the monarchs so unanimously from all as to your imperial highness, and never so fervently as with your present concern for the welfare of the empire.

All the purposes, to which your highness has deigned to devote all the present time of peace, prove beyond dispute your great personal concern, your power, wisdom and happy talent for the completion of great things.

Moreover, when they try to expedite such as your present endeavours, subjects only prove that true duty commands them to give themselves up to their monarch and fatherland, hoping that through such conformity they will show themselves zealous to your majesty.

With such a hope for the royal favour and condescension to her subjects of your imperial highness, I dare to most humbly put forward here my opinion about the establishment in your empire of a legislative, judicial and executive power.

For such undoubtedly most reasonable ideas, your imperial highness will deign to have me in the command of subjects, whose long experience of state affairs will be incomparably more respected in your royal pleasure. And apart from such subjects, the most learned people in Europe consider it their good fortune to serve your highness in such important undertakings, and they can the more foresee what is useful and possible for institution in your empire because of their most sound arguments in jurisprudence and politics.

Therefore my argument about the institutions presented here without such perfection cannot contain in itself any other meaning than that I am trying to the utmost to serve my most gracious monarch with my talent.

However, I must confess that, trying with all my strength, I do not consider myself more than the lowest slave, which I have the good fortune to be for ever

Your imperial highness' most humble
SEMEN DESNITSKII

At the Imperial Moscow University
30 February 1768 [sic]

To make the laws, judge according to the laws and to put the judgement into execution — these three functions constitute the three powers, that is the legislative, judicial and executive power, on which powers depend almost all the administrative arrangements and all the main part of government in the state.[1]

Consequently, the institution of these powers according to the time and place must constitute for those subjects summoned to such business the first object of their discussion, particularly during the presently intended revival in Russia.

Care must be taken with the institution of these powers, that one power does not overstep its limit into another and also that each of these powers should have its supervisors, so that it will always be subject to their concern.

If these powers are first of all happily arranged and delimited by statute, all other regulations which seem necessary may be made in completion of this main business.

In what manner such an establishment may be put into effect, I dare to most humbly submit my plan to your imperial highness.

I. LEGISLATIVE POWER

Nobody in the Russian Empire except monarchs can have this power in its full meaning; however, persons may be called upon by monarchs for such a duty and have as much participation in the legislative power as is now allowed the governing senate, that is they may be allowed as part of their duties with the command and supervision of the Russian monarchs to make decrees anew, correct the old, supplement or abolish them as necessity and the monarch's pleasure demand;[2] beyond this it will be the business of the senators to impose taxes and to lighten them, as necessity demands, to carry on war and observe the conclusion of treaties with neighbouring powers, so that they will not be reprehensible to the fatherland. And since the legislative power is placed higher than all others, so it is necessary that in the Russian senate also the appeal of all cases, which have not been decided in the lower courts, should have its final decision. And when there will be taxes according to the dispensation of the senate and the state account is imposed and collected, the monarchs can then justly order such a governing senate to supervise also the expenditures of the state exchequer, so that all the colleges and schools and universities without exception will be responsible to the governing senate in the expenditure and outlays of the state treasury.

1. *From which and how many people the governing senate may be composed*

For such a size as the Russian empire the senate must consist of at least six or eight hundred persons. These people may be elected with the assent of the monarchs from the landed proprietors in the provinces and counties, also from people involved in commerce and trade, and finally from spiritual and educational institutions, so that each province, county and school should have its representative, defender and intercessor in the legislative power, to whom the circumstances and complaints of his fellow subject citizens would always be known, and through him are presented to the state government for consideration in the senate.

2. *In what way and whence senators should be elected*
In the provinces and counties, senators may be elected with the consent of the monarchs by landlords, smallholders and landed proprietors living in the provinces and counties, so that each proprietor has the honour to have his vote and participation in the election who pays at least fifty roubles poll tax per annum for his land and serfs, and those who pay up to a thousand and more for their own serfs and land under their own name should on no account have more than one vote in the election; to become a candidate for senator may safely be allowed to everybody, as long as he is in a position to live in such a post at his own expense, because senators must not have a quarter-kopeck piece of pay, satisfying themselves with the honour alone and with the privileges that the Russian monarchs choose as a reward for their zealous efforts for the fatherland. And from such an election justice will in fact arise in political life so that only he will have more honour, achievement and participation in government who bears more of a burden in the fatherland, and only he may be a senator who pays more to the sovereign's exchequer and has a capital of at least two thousand per annum.

3. *In what way senators of other ranks may be elected*
From people in commerce and trade those may have a vote in the election of a candidate for senator who pay taxes into the exchequer of up to fifty roubles for the trade allowed them in the fatherland as merchants, and each of the merchants who is in a position to carry out such a duty and to live constantly at the court at his own expense may safely be allowed to announce himself a candidate.

From ecclesiastics, bishops may be allowed to be senators without election if they have in their charge dioceses, for which it will be their function to intercede and present their circumstances and needs in the senate: bishops must also carry out their senatorial duty at their own expense, entrusting the care of their dioceses to their deputies and consistories.

From the universities and various schools, institutions of the sciences and the arts, whichever persons those attached to such places choose may be elected as senator at their expense, and they will intercede for them. The institutions which have such representatives in the governing senate will not ask for guardians as well.

However, how many men and from what places will suffice to be elected as senators may be exactly found out and measured according to an inspection of the provinces, counties and principal towns; and this will become more known through the heralds and gilds, and those places, which the monarch is graciously pleased to point out to have their member in the governing senate, must with gratitude recognise such monarchical permission as an honour and a glory for them.

4. *For how much time the senators may be elected*

When the senators serve their sovereign and fatherland for a long time at their own expense and without pay, there will be for some an immeasurable loss; therefore to elect senators for five years will be sufficient and not at a loss. At the end of this time the monarchs may order the election of new senators in place of the former from the same places, in which election, if some of those who were formerly senators are elected by those having the right to elect and if they themselves do not refuse to serve in the senate for the following five years, it seems there is no reason why such patriots should be prohibited from serving the fatherland a second time. However, it must not be allowed that the same person should become a candidate for senator and be elected three times running, because the advantage will ensue for the fatherland from such a prohibition that many and not just some people will have more of a chance to render their services to the fatherland and to learn government and jurisprudence in the office of senator.

5. *In what way the senators should sit and carry out business*

Senators elected and summoned in this manner to one and the same duty, that is to serve the sovereign and the fatherland (which calling they must under a sworn oath carry out with all possible effort and the utmost understanding), must all be allowed, the good of the fatherland advises, to have an equal free vote and to sit together in the senate; the affairs which the monarch will be pleased to order them to decide should always be decided in the senate by a majority of the votes. After this has been done, each decision should be given to the monarch and the final command awaited from him. And the governing senate should henceforth not undertake and make any enactment without the permission and order of the monarchs in Russia. In Great Britain until both parliaments agree with the king, in France until the secretary and the parliament sign, till then no projected legislation can be put into effect and have the force of law. In Russia, however, the monarchical condition and the safety of the fatherland demand the enactment of regulations completely opposite to these states, that is until the monarchical assent and confirmation is received nothing can be promulgated and have the force of a decree. For such a precaution the monarch may order the Russian governing senate to elect annually a president, whose function will be to present to the monarch matters for his decision. However, the monarch must allow privileges and ranks to such patriots as it pleases him; and for the glory and greatness of the Russian empire it would not be superfluous if the Russian monarchs ordered in Moscow and St. Petersburg the construction of special buildings for the sessions and residence of the Russian governing senate.

6. *Objection to this plan with a refutation of it*

From the aforementioned it is evident that by this plan, nobles, people of various ranks, both spiritual and lay equally, in the office of senator, will be equal without any distinction, which may produce indignation between those summoned to the senatorial duty; particularly to those of spiritual rank this equality will perhaps seem strange.

As for the spiritual rank, it cannot in its wise humility consider it unreasonable or indecent to sit in the senate with people of the first class present. Since also in the reasoning of this plan, some people cannot be like the Russian citizens of the first class, the others will have only the vote in the election of candidates as senators. Moreover, one pastor with such a large flock cannot so thoroughly look after it, as six or eight hundred in the senate. And from the feeble efforts of one placed over many, multitudes of people can stray and become reprehensible to themselves and to the fatherland.

There is no reason why the nobility should not agree with people of various ranks together in session of the senate. They have no private interest in anything, but the prosperity and welfare of the whole fatherland must always be kept in view as a principal rule. However, all disagreements and discord that may occur between secular and spiritual senators could be appropriately erased in one word by the monarch of all the Russias, who in the Russian church and empire is the autocrat and the one supervisor and judge, on whose orders the senate depends and in whose sole command it will be forever.

To refuse, being in a position to serve in harmonious obedience to the sovereign and the fatherland, may justly be considered as such a digression from virtuous behaviour that those who eschew the senatorial rank must be ashamed before God and the whole world. Our fatherland constitutes a certain whole, of which we all consider ourselves separate members, and so it is considered an unforgiveable sin by peoples if anybody living in the fatherland considers himself separate from it. Of good and bad everybody must remember only that which concerns the whole fatherland, to which everybody is obliged for whatever he has. The true son of the fatherland, when he spills his sweat and blood for the safety of the fatherland, with such services he only gives up to the fatherland what duty commands. It bears him, brings him up and feeds him for this. With the sanctity of its laws it defends him from domestic insults, and with its strength and weapons – from enemy attacks. The fatherland makes him famous and gives him position, honour and consideration. It rewards his services and avenges his insults and, finally, like the assiduous mother to her children, it attempts to confirm his happiness as unshakeably as it is possible for mortals to be happy. Therefore, everybody summoned and elected to such a duty is in conscience as much obliged to serve the whole fatherland in it – this seems superfluous to prove more.

II JUDICIAL POWER

From the aforementioned plan it stands to reason, that the legislative power will be composed and assembled from the whole Russian empire in one place, that is in the capital town as its centre; the judicial power, on the other hand, demands no less that it be distributed throughout the whole empire thus:

1. *In which places in Russia the judicial power must always be present*

The size of the Russian empire, the speedy decision of affairs, and still more the peace and quiet so necessary in the fatherland demand that in Russia at least in eight places a certain number of expert judges should always be present, that is: in Riga, in St. Petersburg, in Tobol'sk, in Novgorod, in Moscow, in Kazan, in Orenburg, in Glukhov and, if possible, in some place on the Polish borders.

2. *Of what persons in these places the judicial power may consist*

For the speedy consideration of cases and for their just decision, the judicial power must in all the aforementioned places consist of twelve people, in whose number must be included a general-advocate and four criminal general-judges. The other seven must be general-judges of civil and criminal affairs in the place where all twelve judges will be together.

3. *Which duty must be entrusted to the general-advocate*

He may be in the court a state prosecutor or plaintiff, whose task will be to be present in the criminal and civil court and to see that everything in detail may be judged according to the decrees. Beyond this, the task of the general-advocate will be to impose a conviction on all the guilty and to summons to the court in the name of the Russian monarch without exception all those properly accused of theft, brigandage, murder and other criminal deeds, all of whom it will be his function to order to keep on trial and then in prisons and fortresses until they have borne the punishment suitable to their cases according to law.

4. *The function which the four general criminal judges may have*

The function of these persons may be, firstly, the same as that of the other seven general judges, that is their business will be to sit and judge civil and criminal affairs together in the place appointed; beyond this, the function of these four judges will be to go with the general-advocate to the county towns belonging to the province twice a year and two together, and they must stay in each town six days and judge criminal cases, because civil cases may be transferred without difficulty from all towns to the chief court of the province, where all twelve judges will be present.

5. *In what way the judges must judge criminal and civil cases*

Civil cases they must judge according to the laws and contracts and, if the laws do not suffice — according to equity and truth,[3] criminal — by the testimony of eye-witnesses.

And both the former and the latter must be judged publicly in the presence of outsiders, and everybody's testimony must be submitted under a sworn obligation, and everything that witnesses say under such an obligation, the judges must in turn say to the clerk, so that he may write down for them what has been said by the witnesses; and a criminal case, once started in court, should be finished in one session, although it continues twenty hours or even more; and apart from this, supervision for greater care in the conviction of the guilty and for the clear correctness of the court would be increased, if the Russian monarchs would be pleased to enact after the English example the selection from forty outsiders of fifteen jurors to assist and support the judges in the investigation of criminal and civil affairs; such people may at the discretion and choice of the judges be elected for each court from all the inhabitants of the town where the court is held, and only for the time until the court is finished. For this the fifteen men must be spectators and witnesses of the whole investigation of the cases, and their function must be to say under a sworn oath after the investigation of the whole case, whether the accused is guilty or not, and after this the function of the judges will be by their votes or the majority of the votes to pronounce judgement and order it to be put into execution. Beyond this, it would not be bad if such judges were ordered to print all decisions of criminal and civil cases and to publish them, because through this arrangement such an outstanding success may be brought about in justice that the judge will be forced to act in the court with great care. And besides, reading various decisions, people will unwittingly learn more of what they must fear in their life and property.

6. *In what knowledge and subjects the judges must be skilled*

The skill and knowledge necessary for a judge depend:

(i) On the characteristics of his ideas about what is said to be good and bad in society.

(ii) Such knowledge may be incomparably increased by the study of many examples of court cases.

The first guide, which shows what the characteristics of our ideas consist of, is moral philosophy, natural jurisprudence and, apart from these, the study of human nature, which will be made known more from reading and the observations of writers about the various governments of peoples than from scholastic metaphysical arguments.

The second means of furnishing our minds with sufficient examples of legal cases is the study of such a system in which can clearly be seen all the examples of decisions, and beyond this, the basis and completion of government. For this there is no better system than the Roman laws. Therefore before entering such a duty, judges must be exercised in moral philosophy, natural jurisprudence, in Roman laws, and apart from these subjects, they must know in detail and skilfully interpret the laws of their fatherland,[4] so that having learned everything and being examined in everything and attested, at first by professors of the faculty of jurisprudence and afterwards by the faculty of law, those intending to be judges must demonstrate their calling in legal practice for at least five years, at the end of which they must themselves and through their friends recommend themselves to the monarch for creation as judges, and so that nobody apart from the monarch can create judges under any pretext, the advantage of the fatherland demands that this too should be strictly enacted.

7. *For how much time and on what pay the judges may be instituted*

So that the judge may prescribe justice and truth for all without regard to anybody, make him not subject to any threats and not dependent on anybody to such an extent that nobody will be frightened of the justice and severity of his court, which cannot properly be done otherwise until the monarchs are pleased to enact that a judge, once created, should be a judge and in his post for life, and besides that full authority should be given him to judge everybody without exception, so that nobody should be allowed to make an appeal against him to anybody, unless in a case where he obviously convicts somebody against the law. And then the advocate or the guilty person may be allowed an appeal against the judge to the governing senate, where he must be subjected to a fine at the discretion of the monarch or to punishment. And in order that the judge may live according to his rank and dignity, therefore the general-advocate and the four criminal judges may be allowed pay of two thousand six hundred rubles per annum for each, and the other seven general judges — two thousand rubles per annum each. The general-advocate and the four judges referred to must travel at their own expense to the county towns for the judgement of the guilty and for the expeditious settlement of cases.

It would not be superfluous with this, if the monarchs were pleased to order the construction of proper buildings for the session and residence of the judges in the provinces where they will be, and in the county towns — courts with prisons and apartments for the visiting judges.

However, the monarch may allow the judges the clothing, insignia and privileges which he deems necessary.

I must confess here that all the rules, according to which the judges must act and in what way to impose convictions and summon the guilty to court, cannot be made more comprehensively, unless the plan for criminal and civil justice devised here is presented openly to all the deputies in the Commission, for which I am always most humbly at the command of your imperial highness. But this, perhaps, may seem superfluous. Therefore, I most humbly beg to put forward to your imperial highness for consideration what most importantly concerns the perfection of the judicial power, that is that you would deign to enact for greater prudence:

(i) That judges should only have the authority to judge everybody without exception, and that the Russian monarch alone should have the right to pardon whomsoever he pleases, for which the monarch may appoint a secretary and a chancellery, whose function would be to present the case of the convicted and the punishment arranged by the court to the monarch for his pleasure, for which six weeks will be enough to allow the convicted time to confess and await the conviction.

(ii) When such care is instituted in such an important court, for which the judge himself no less than the summoned to court will be bound by the laws, the very correctness of justice and the welfare of the fatherland may the more convince the legislator of the necessity everywhere in the Russian empire for everybody without exception to be punished for his guilt, as for example, a murderer — by death, a thief — by public degradation and the most dishonourable punishment and so on.

8. *Objection to this proposal*

Indeed, such severity of the laws by which the guilty are sometimes obliged to satisfy the court and the laws of the fatherland not otherwise than with life itself cannot be demonstrated to be anything but insupportable and burdensome. Learned advisers will not fail to make use of strong objections to it, contending that in so far as nobody apart from God is in a position to give life to a man, nobody has the right to take it away. Beyond this, many noble and aristocratic families demur from such severity of the laws, presenting their family and their blood as worthy of compassion and exception from such severity. – As far as the first objection is concerned, it is completely unfounded and comes to learned people from the incorrectness of their arguments; such syllogisms are irrelevant in jurisprudence. The monarch or by his order the judge who punishes murderers and villains dangerous to the fatherland does only that which God and nature command: to take an eye for an eye, a tooth for a tooth and a life for a life – was God's law and is sufficiently natural. Nature, which flows down from God to man, always draws us to such a revenge for evil, just as with us through Christianity and humanity there is no goodness which is not created by goodness. If the death penalty is moderated according to the case and does not exceed the limit of severity, each impartial spectator will have kind feelings for the guilty and [nevertheless] condemn him until he is in the place where the evil occurred and suffers the appropriate punishment with a hand and a weapon like he himself used for evil. A true proof of this is the common voice of the people, which in such cases usually says: "The rogue deserves much more than that! He should die a thousand deaths" and so on. With the death penalty care must be taken that severity does not exceed limits, because in the contrary case natural kindness concerning the punishment inflicted on the guilty will turn impartial witnesses to pity and the condemnation of the judges themselves, from which the death penalty may lose that success, which the government must try to create so positively, that the guilty will be condemned both by themselves and by the whole people and not be able to expect pity from anybody. – Moreover the aristocratic and high-born nobles, convicted in criminal and homicidal cases, will ask for the exemption of themselves from such severity and sanctity of the laws, so that all the salutary laws will be made ineffective in the fatherland, which they, as sons of the fatherland, cannot want. To make the high-born dishonoured and defamed before the whole people as rabble and commonalty will be a limitless punishment, because the honour of the high-born is placed on a level with life, so that in the contemporary enlightened European peoples the honour of the high-born is given great esteem even in the most extreme circumstances; for this reason they do not condemn the high-born to be bound to a pillory and publicly dishonoured, and the high-born would rather choose for themselves a double punishment than a single dishonour. If the lowest officer is to be punished with a stick or a sword, in such a case he will say that cattle should be struck with a stick and the officer with a sword, which is a sufficient proof of the whole distinction necessary for the high-born from the commonalty in punishment, that is nobles may be fined, sent to exile and executed, but not publicly dishonoured.

III. EXECUTIVE POWER
Since it is the last, this power must depend on the higher powers more than any of the others. And for this the procedure needs to be enacted in the fatherland that those having executive power should henceforth not undertake anything important by themselves without public censure by the judges.

1. *To whom the executive power may properly be entrusted*
At the pleasure of the monarch this power may be allowed and entrusted to sheriffs in the provinces and only the most important of the county towns, so that one sheriff should not depend on another, but they should all depend on the monarch himself, who would alone have the authority to appoint them to such a position. This direction is necessary so that great people should not be able to overthrow him for unpleasant severity occasioned them by the sheriff in the course of his duties.

And so that the sheriff should not sometimes needlessly harm the innocent, prudence demands a decree to the effect that he be subject to the twelve judges in the chief provincial court, who must at each trial publicly ask those present, if there is any complaint about the sheriff or any offence caused by him. And if there is any complaint or offence to anybody from him, the judges must report it to the governing senate, where the sheriff will be subject to a fine and punishment at the monarch's pleasure.

2. *Which duty may be entrusted to the sheriff*
His duty must generally consist of keeping peace and quiet in the places entrusted to him, that is to take thieves, brigands and the like to prison and to report them to the general-advocate, who will impose conviction on them, ordering them to appear in the name of the monarch and to prepare themselves at a certain time for trial in the county town or the chief provincial court.

Beyond this his duty will be — to keep the guilty in prison and to execute them in the place ordered by the judges. Finally, the duty of the sheriff may be to collect the poll tax and duties from the landed proprietors, which the governing senate will prescribe in the county or province entrusted to him.

And because for the execution of such business and for the careful supervision of it a certain number of people is necessary to help the sheriff, therefore the sheriffs must be allowed in their provinces a hundred infantrymen and twenty cavalrymen, who must exclusively be in the charge of the sheriff, and he would always be responsible for their misdemeanours. In a county town fifty men will suffice the sheriff for the execution of his duty.

Payment of up to six hundred rubles may be allowed the provincial and county sheriffs, and if possible, houses should be constructed for them at state expense.

In capital towns, such as Saint Petersburg and Moscow, payment of a thousand rubles per annum may be allowed the sheriffs and beyond this suitable houses should be built for them. Soldiers should also be allowed to the sheriffs in such towns as necessity demands. And, apart from this institution, order, peace and security in the capital towns demand that they should be divided into squads, such as, for example, Moscow — into twelve squads, and they should have in each squad an officer with one hundred and eighty infantrymen and twenty cavalrymen permanently at a place constructed for each squad with a watch-tower, a prison, a firehose and English fire barrels, whose effect in a fire is unfailing and indisputable.[5]

It will be the duty of the infantrymen in each squad constantly to keep watch in the streets and to observe peace and quiet in the places assigned to them; it will be the duty of the cavalrymen to go on patrol, to catch runaways, thieves, brigands and criminally convicted people escaping from jail. The duty of the officers appointed to the squads will will be to keep a strict watch on the soldiers and to order the guilty brought to them to be kept in prison until further orders in the report from the sheriff, whose duty will also be to detail those accused and arraigned for murder, theft, revolts and other criminal affairs to the general-advocate and to bring them to the judges for conviction, to carry out which his duty will be to punish and execute the convicted in the places assigned by the court. Beyond this it will be the duty of the sheriff in the capital towns to see that everything is in strict good order in his squads, for the supervision of whom he must himself have a general round and tour of all squads at least once a week. And in the contrary case, when the sheriff neglects or is slow to carry out his duty, for such carelessness he must be subjected to strict punishment, firstly before the judges, and later in the governing senate at the monarch's pleasure to a fine and punishment. For such an institution two thousand soldiers in each of the capital towns and eight hundred in each town will be enough. Retired soldiers and officers may be used for such duties, only not the completely old and infirm, and Moscow and St. Petersburg inhabitants will not refuse to construct barracks and stone buildings for them by squads, being convinced sufficiently that in the contrary case they will have soldiers permanently in their houses, and to send their household people on watch will become incomparably more expensive and cause more difficulties and disquiet than such construction which, once completed, will always serve soldiers and watchmen. However, it would not be superfluous, if it were granted to order to build in all provincial towns and the most important county towns secure barracks and quarters for the sheriff's soldiers in residences of the sheriff, so that the soldiers in them may always be before his eyes and would not burden his underlings with dishonourable billeting so that the town inhabitants may enthusiastically agree to this at their own expense and beyond this not omit, if it be commanded, to order firepumps for these towns for defence from fire, from which they will all everywhere suffer so much without such machines, whose upkeep, care and permanent readiness will be entrusted to the sheriff, and which relieve and deliver many people from fire.

In supplement to judicial and executive power

And so that the least offences will not be let past without punishment and satisfaction, but not be any trouble for the chief court, for the decision in the county towns of offences which will not cause those suffering them more than a loss of twenty five rubles and which will also not be criminal, may it be enacted that they may be decided by landlords, smallholders and merchants of that county, for the establishment of which the monarch may in such places order the landlords, smallholders and merchants to have their chancellery and to sit in it six men four times a month and to decide cases of minor importance, not allowing them to make an appeal to a higher court. By insults of small importance they must mean those which arise through the ignorance or negligence of people, such as for example, if somebody takes a horse from another and ruins it, or if somebody's cattle, going on to somebody else's fields, will cause loss to another, and so on. Beyond this the care of roads and proper construction in towns may be ordered by such a chancellery.

Such an enactment may be allowed and put into practice only in unimportant towns in the counties, and contrary to this, the capital, provincial and most important commercial towns must all be the concern of the civic power for which, although I did not promise it in the foreword, I must nevertheless give a plan here.

IV. CIVIC POWER

This power must be entrusted to the people who live in towns and who carry on most of their business in them. Consequently, such power may be allowed to citizens, and still more to merchants and craftsmen.

1. In which towns and from what people the civic power must be formed

In capital towns for the multitude of affairs and the speedy dispatch of them, the municipal power must consist of seventy three persons, that is of eighteen nobles living in town, and of fifty five merchants, who altogether constituting seventy three men, may be divided into six departments, so that each department may consist of twelve persons, that is of nine merchants of the first gild and three nobles, and the remaining one of the seventy three must be elected president of the civic power by a general majority of votes.

(i) The function of the first department will be to carry out business in the town connected with bills of exchange, and so special regulations or a law of the governing senate may be ordered.

(ii) The function of the second department will be to observe the cheapness of the comestible supplies being sold in the town, that is to carefully watch that everything in the shops and at the markets be sold at a known price and with the legal state weight and measure. And besides this – the function of the second department will be – to eradicate speculators and profiteers, who make the price of articles more expensive and cause the inhabitants an unnecessary loss and difficulties in upkeep.

(iii) The third department will have the supervision of civic architecture, which must be strictly observed in the town according to the plan prescribed by the governing senate so that the town will not to the contrary reveal the oppressiveness and absurdity of disordered construction and dilapidated ramshackle buildings.

(iv) The fourth department will supervise the repair of roads and canals, necessary for the avoidance of dirt in the town; the duty of this department will also be to see that street lights properly arranged burn brightly at a fixed time and that the roads in the places surrounding the town should always be kept up.

(v) The business of the fifth department will be to collect those taxes from the inhabitants and tradespeople, on the articles and at the rate that the governing senate will allow them for the municipal use of the civic power.

(vi) The function of the sixth and last department will be to decide cases of minor importance, which to those involved in them will cause a loss of no more than twenty five rubles and which will also not be criminal.

By arbitration of this department must be decided all disagreements and insults such as those between cabmen, cooks and tradespeople come into town. The duty of the president in all these departments will be to be present at the meetings and to see that all members will be in court at a fixed time and carry out business in a short time. And because the departments of the civic power will carry on all their business by the regulations prescribed to them by the senate, appeals should therefore not be allowed against these departments, except in the obvious instance when the civic power infringes the senate decree prescribed for it, and then the injured by the civic power may be allowed to complain to the judicial power, where the department acting against the prescribed rules must undergo a strict punishment and fine at the discretion of the twelve chief judges.

2. *For how much time and at what expense the members of the civic power must be elected*

When those taking on themselves civic power are town inhabitants, of which some derive their living from the town and others are consumers there, it will thus not be disadvantageous for each inhabitant in turn to serve in civic duty at his own expense for two years. And if any of the inhabitants or merchants refuses to serve in such civic duty, such unpatriotic and unwilling people should pay a fine of two hundred and fifty rubles for disobedience and obstinacy.

3. *Of how many and which people the civic power must consist in other towns*

In provincial and outstanding commercial county towns the civic power must be entrusted to twelve men, in the number of whom must be seven merchants and five nobles, town inhabitants or living near the town.

The duty of these men in provincial and outstanding county towns must be as prescribed for the civic power in the capital towns, with the sole change, that in provincial and other towns members of the civic power should all sit together, not dividing into departments and carry out civic power together, electing one of themselves president.

However in all towns as in the capitals, the members of the civic power may carry out their duties for two years in turn at their own expense, and for disobedience should be subjected to the above fine.

The insignia and dress for the distinction of the civic power from other powers, equally the building, the monarch may allow as he pleases.

The public buildings for the session of the senators, the judges of the magistracy and the sheriffs, must be, particularly in the capital towns, magnificent, safe and built in the centre of town, within which buildings it would not be superfluous if the monarchs were pleased to order to have for the senate, judges, lawyers and the magistrate a general magnificent church, to which all such instituted powers should go once each Sunday, at least some members, as the good order of religion and welfare of the fatherland demand, and besides the members of all the powers should go to such a church in a parade with their insignia and the clothing prescribed for them, each power have before it its herald, bearing before him the regalia, even to places appointed specially for each power in the church; of this also the affirmation of the faith demands the strict enactment.

Now in Russia it is not the practice for the secular nor even for the spiritual authorities to go into the public church and to stand visibly there before all. Nearly all the bishops and archimandrites have their private churches, nobody sees them in the public church, except when they are conducting a service there; when they are not doing so, they go through the permanent doors to the altar, and nobody sees them. And how much the affirmation of faith depends on the example of the spiritual and the secular powers being present publicly in church demands no proof.

For such an arrangement the Russian monarchs with the governing senate may in time take into consideration the reform of the church calendar, so that all holidays may take place and be celebrated on Sunday and so that everybody may try to keep the Sabbath day holy with such reverence, the public drinking houses and taverns should not be open on it before the end of mass and nobody except the monarch should be allowed private churches. Military schools and educational institutions may have their special churches, equally there should be special places in them for the attendance of those in charge and their subordinates.

As the most humble and least slave presenting this to the royal consideration of your imperial majesty, I must confess that in such a short plan it is impossible to describe in detail everything that concerns such institutions. Your imperial highness, with your most perfect talent, will incomparably deign to manage what is most useful and timely for reform and institution in your empire. I have tried here to the utmost of my understanding to suggest but a short and general idea about the institution of these powers in your so wide dominions, thinking that if it would be your royal pleasure to order the Commission and the advisers to set about, firstly, the discussion and institution of these powers, the so useful intentions for the human race undertaken by your highness may the more quickly and promptly be put into effect. All the felicity of subjects and sovereigns consists of the skilful institution of these powers. It is true that the legislative power is properly placed first by all peoples; however on the judicial, executive and civic powers depends all the fulfilment of the laws, without which the best and wisest enactments would be ineffective. Many peoples have found out by experience that it is better not to have laws than, having them, not to carry them out, because from the non-fulfilment of laws that weakness in government is born which many thoughtlessly also ascribe to all other state institutions. But this also may not be unknown to your royal consideration, and so it remains only for your subjects to ask the Supreme Being for uninterrupted happiness and success to your majesty in the business undertaken and to await with patience the happy outcome of all your wishes and blessed intentions. However deign now to undertake the work so worthy of your great talents, about which the monarchs and top authorities in Europe are already convinced. Besides those scattered in the northern country and other lawless and helpless people in the middle of icy and burning climes will owe to your majesty such gratitude, when by your present revival and the striving of your enthusiastic educational institutions will come such a blessed condition in which they will see the true light, showing them of what the sanctity of the laws, the safety of society, the true confession of faith and the recompense of labour consist. Neighbouring powers, seeing such joyful transformation of your dominion, will not fail to commit your reign to undying glory and seek your bountiful friendship, protection and alliance, binding themselves equally to serve your majesty in all undertakings.

This sincere unanimity, so deserving to your majesty from the whole world, will quickly pour out from all hearts in your power with particular zeal for the fatherland, with particular harmony in the recognition and celebration of your virtuous intention and undertaking.

I, Semen Desnitskii, Doctor of Laws in the Imperial Moscow University, composed this.

30 February 1768 [sic]

Desnitskii's footnotes (not numbered in the original)

1.   Many political authors (and particularly Baron de Montesquieu in his work "On the Spirit of the Laws") have written of these three powers as they have been established in various states in the course of their affairs. And as these powers may be established according to the time and place for the expeditious dispatch of state business, the legislator himself may know more about them.
       In this plan I have tried to the utmost of my understanding to adapt the establishment of such powers to the present flourishing condition of the Russian monarchy.

2.   To make, supplement, amend or repeal laws – the circumstances will demand this in time, when the state begins to come into an even greater perfection and when commerce and customs duties begin to rise. In states, which had still not yet reached great perfection the laws were proportionately simple and few. All the laws of the Romans were accommodated in twelve tables. However, because of the long-term duration of the state, those same Romans turned out to be so extensive in their laws, that those which were formerly contained in twelve slabs in the end could not be kept even in two thousand books. In Great Britain, where the laws are now in great perfection, just an

abridgement of the laws alone takes up twenty-five books. Many learned persons, not reasoning that such a multitude of laws is demanded by the natural rise of peoples in government, have begun to abridge the institutions and laws of Rome and other countries, when a contrary course is demonstrated by the experience of all states. It cannot be otherwise, the more peoples rise, become enlightened and enter a higher perfection, the more laws they require. This in turn requires an exact and generally known arrangement of the laws for all landlords, town inhabitants and all their property. And on the other hand effrontery, infringement, imposition and oppression will everywhere be occurring without punishment. Consequently, for this and many other state affairs the governing senate must be made up from the whole empire and must be in constant attendance to the monarchs for ever.

3. To judge according to truth and equity in circumstances when the law does not suffice, because it is impossible to foresee and delimit by the laws all eventualities in any state, consequently demands through necessity in such unforseen circumstances that judges should be allowed to judge according to conscience and equity. How far such permission should be given to judges must also be enacted with care. About this one lord of justice Kames in Scotland has written in more detail a whole book: Lord Kames's "Equity".

4. All the subjects in which a judge must be learned cannot be described here in detail. When a judge enters on his duties he will himself find out to a greater extent of what his knowledge and practice should consist. But now it can be asserted demonstrably about him in general that he must have a full university education. For this because of the size of the Russian state schools might be set up in due course in all places where civil and criminal chief justices will be present, likewise law faculties with the libraries necessary for advocates. However the judge, like the craftsman, will be more skilled in his business and knowledge, the more he has in his head the various examples necessary for his profession. And therefore he must know history, and various languages such as for example Latin, German, French and English, so that he may with the help of these read various systems of law and deepen his knowledge and skill in legal affairs.

    The institution of advocates is necessary so that cases might be decided with great care and equity. Many think that advocates cause great difficulties in the court with their contention about words. However, in many states it has been ascertained by experience that without arguments in court there is no way of achieving equity. Equity and prudence in the courts demand that it should be strictly enacted that in the governing senate in the chief civil and criminal courts advocates alone should plead. In the lower courts, for example in the magistracy and in the chancelleries of the counties and the sheriffs, notaries and attorneys may plead.

5. These barrels of machines are called "Mr. Godfrey's machines or barrels". They are of various sizes in weight, from five pounds up to fifty, full of water, and diluted with chemical anti-phlogiston. I. shall communicate without fail the tests and actions of these machines to the Economic Society in the month of May, in a dissertation about the establishment of agriculture in Russia on a better basis. These barrels may be ordered or subscribed for in England at least for the capital towns and for the fleet. And apart from this it would not be superfluous to order for a year from Britain,

a mechanic for the manufacture of the new copper fire hoses. Such a man is Mr. Watt, who is skilled in mechanics, mathematics and natural philosophy, and who, having come to Russia with his workers, could for forty or fifty thousand rubles make machines in one year of sufficient quantity and of the highest quality from state materials.

Appendices (in summary)

Appendix I　　　　*Third Division – On the Lower Order*
This order has now in Russia a satisfactory situation. One part has the rights and advantages appropriate to it, the other is deprived of all benefits and has no property at all. To the first part belong smallholders, farmer-soldiers and the land militia, also certain categories of state peasants and tribute-paying peasants. To the second belong the court, church and landlord peasants. The Commission must now perpetuate this difference so that order is maintained continually in its work. The first part is to have its rights and advantages examined and confirmed, including non-enserfment, property and testament. The second part could not receive rights and advantages without the destruction of the peace of the state, but abuses of these people can be curtailed if sensible institutions are set up, with the permission of the landlords and proper guarantee of their interests. This would be to the profit of the landlords, as can be seen in Livonia, where the farmer has advantages but is no less obedient to the lord. The principles of the Instruction must be the basis for an exact arrangement, as could be borrowings from other lands. It is against humanity, ruinous to the state and harmful to the landlords to sell peasants retail apart from their families or without land. A committee of the Commission could consider household serfs – their selection by the landlords themselves to the satisfaction of the peasant commune and families and without the exactions of the stewards. Emancipated serfs are not be enserfed again.

Appendix II　　　　*Spiritual Administration*
Long-lasting traditions and the Synod arrangement of Peter the Great are not to be disturbed. But four sets of propositions are set out concerning in turn church officials; the good order of church buildings; the clerical supervision and control of secular people; and the upkeep of the priesthood and of church buildings.
　　A spiritual committee is to be set up to deal with these propositions.

Appendix III　　　　*Letter A of the Second Part of the Plan*
The nationalities consist of all three kinds of people, that is upper, middle and lower. They have a military function, defending the fatherland from external enemies. They are either Cossacks or various non-nomadic peoples. They have no parallel in Europe, but are very useful for Russia. Their agriculture and their education are to be encouraged. There should be a committee on these "military inhabitants".

Appendix IV　　　　*On Financial Legislation*
This should concern expenditure and income. Expenditure is of four

kinds. The first is the upkeep of the sovereign and his establishment, his rewards and endowments, the second is that of internal order, including police and the courts. The third concerns communications, education, the arts and sciences. The fourth and most important kind of expenditure is on the armed forces and their supplies.

Five questions can be answered concerning income.

1. On which objects should taxes be levied? On people (poll tax), immovable property (land and buildings, England being a good example of the first), comestibles (but not on grain, and not advisable on salt), luxuries such as liquor and tobacco, tariffs (but not internal, and to be paid by vendor, not purchaser), and transactions (such as sales and court fines — less reliable but easier than others).

2. How can taxes be made lightest for the people? If everybody is taxed, and mostly on luxuries; best of all if taxes are scaled with geometric progression. Tax farming is bad in all countries, and if necessary, must be strictly supervised. Monopolies and internal customs are to avoided.

3. How can expenses of collection be reduced? If salt is carried by water as much as possible, landlords or villages conduct the collection of poll tax, salt and liquor tax arrangements are improved (with abolition or at least reform of liquor tax-farming).

4. How can taxes be made reliable? If insignificant taxes are abolished, poll tax arrears in certain counties are explained and reduced, if canal construction is developed and liquor taxes are regularised.

5. How should income be administered? By a unified authority, a committee on state finances or income.

From the edition of A.A. Zheludkov in S.A. Pokrovskii ed., *Proizvedeniia progressivnykh myslitelei: vtoraia polovina XVIII veka*, M., 1959.

6. A. Ia. Polenov on the Serf Condition of the Peasants, c.1768

INTRODUCTION

Aleksei Iakovlevich Polenov was born the son of a guardsman in Moscow Province in the year 1738. At the age of eleven, he entered the gymnasium of the Academy of Sciences, and, in 1754, its university, studying jurisprudence for the most part and also helping with the translation into Russian of the Lithuanian Statute. In 1762, he was sent to the University of Strasburg, where he specialised in jurisprudence, but did some philosophy, classics and history as well. In 1766, Polenov transferred to the University of Göttingen, where he continued jurisprudence as well as history. He was recalled in the summer of 1767 to help with the work of the Legislative Commission, although he seems to have concentrated his energies on his essay on serfdom and on an edition of the Nikon Chronicle. He also worked at the Academy on translations of such varied writers as Montesquieu, Frederick II and Theophrastus. In 1771, he left the Academy for the Senate, where he was a secretary in charge of typography; among the decrees he saw through the press was the Charter of Nobility. During his years at the Senate, Polenov received ranks, titles and other rewards. In 1793, he moved to the State Loan Bank, and from 1796 to 1798, he worked on the codification of criminal laws. At about the same time, he was engaged in writing the history of the Knights of St. John of Jerusalem, a subject close to the heart of the Emperor Paul, but the history was never published because of the forcible removal of Paul in 1801. Just before this, Polenov had gone into retirement; he died in 1816.

"On the Serf Condition of the Peasants in Russia" was submitted as an entry for a prize essay competition sponsored in the mid-1760s by the newly founded Free Economic Society under the strong influence of the Empress herself. It was numbered 148 out of 164, and identified also by its motto, "Good morals are worth more than good laws". Some of the members of the prize committee considered it worthy of a place in the competition, but others thought that it contained "many inordinately strong statements unsuitable for this condition",[1] and should be awarded a prize only if Polenov carried out revisions. Polenov received a gold medal and twelve crowns as recognition for the excellence of his work, but "On the Serf Condition" was not published until nearly a hundred years had elapsed and serfdom had been abolished. Various intellectual influences on

Polenov's essay have been suggested, among them Helvetius, Holbach, Montesquieu, Morelli, Rousseau and Voltaire. Undoubtedly, his years at Strasburg and Göttingen had exposed him to all the ideas then circulating among progressive thinkers in France and Germany. It is also worth noting that Polenov, who equates Russian serfdom with slavery in general, was writing at a time when the abolitionist movement was taking on ideological shape in Western Europe and in the Western Hemisphere.

The prize essay competition constituted the first public discussion in Russia of the institution of serfdom. Some of the members of the Free Economic Society were concerned that it "should not in the least spoil the order and peace of the state." They decided to ask the Empress for permission before announcing the results, deeming such a precaution necessary since the competition concerned "fundamental state arrangements," about which "without specific leave from the highest authority" it would not be fitting for private individuals or groups to give their opinions. The members of the competition committee took the fearful decision "not to translate into Russian or to publish any of the pieces concerning this matter, not even that which merits the award." A "short extract" only might be given in Russian, excluding everything that "might create a negative impression, or serve as the occasion for violent and harmful thoughts." Some thought it would be better if the successful essays were published in foreign languages and in foreign lands, with the society ordering just a few copies for itself. Only two members voted for publication in Russian translation of the winning entry, even though Catherine said that she did not find in that essay "anything which could not be published."[2] If she had not exerted her influence, the essay would not have got into print, and the competition would have degenerated into farce.

Polenov's submission may be examined in context if we take a glance at the prize winner and at some of the other entries. The top award of a thousand crowns went to Bearde de l'Abaye, a Doctor of Laws at Aachen University. His suggestion was that the serfs might be enabled to acquire landed property, but gradually and on a scale so small that it would never be sufficient even for subsistence purposes. If such a modest innovation were made, the serfs would no longer think of running away, but rather of using what land they had and of renting more from their landlords, even at high prices. And the result situation would be very much to the liking of the landlords, in de l'Abaye's view: "The rich, not being troubled by constant supervision, receive their income punctually and in considerable amounts. . . . It is a pleasure to see your dog following you everywhere . . . can it be compared with the burdensome labour of leading a bear?"[3]

Such views as these, it will be recalled, were considered too dangerous for publication by all but two members of the competition committee.

69

More to their taste for content if not for style would probably have been the observations of "A man who is ungrammatical and has not read any history since birth." Good landlords, this author argued, would not take movable property away from their serfs, and might even lend it to some of them who were too poor to acquire it for themselves. But immovable property could not be granted, for all the lands worked by their peasants and the houses occupied by them were the hereditary, granted or purchased property of the landlords. Nor could freedom be given to the serfs, as it had been in foreign lands, for peasants would then become even lazier and more prone to flight than they already were. Moreover, other consequences would include: "endless lawsuits and Their Excellencies the Field Marshals . . . who command the glorious Russian army would be compelled to petition the commissars for their brave lads but we in Russia have more brave lads than in foreign parts because the peasants are literate there and in Russia, with God's care, even the priests are not all that literate. The landlords teach their serfs not only folk-dancing, but also carpentry and part-singing." Abolition would become possible in Russia only when:

"Russia becomes as populous as the kingdom of Holland, when our priests are as literate as foreign priests, the nobles such sharp-witted fellows as the English and the French, the peasants know their ABC and are consequently honest and obey more the wrath of God and go to church more often than to the drinking houses, do not stave in barges on the Volga, and our rabble has a better understanding of foreign crafts, and becomes more intelligent."[4]

While essays as negative as this — if more coherently compiled — were in the large majority, Polenov was not quite alone in his decided affirmative, for several entries went along with his on the question of property rights for the peasantry and therefore approached however distantly the dreaded topic of emancipation. Among these were some from abroad, from Voltaire (although this survives only in part) and the minor philosopher Marmontel, and some from within the Russian Empire, from Johann Georg Eisen von Schwarzenberg, a Lutheran pastor resident in the Baltic provinces, the mathematician Leonhard Euler, who lived in St. Petersburg for many years, and No. 71, whose identity is unknown. Polenov's essay is translated here as a representative of the more progressive responses to the prize competition, because it is the most complete of those available to us by native Russians. A coherent analysis and set of proposals, it foreshadows many of the points put forward in the debate leading up to the Emancipation of 1861 and in the Emancipation edicts themselves as well.

Footnotes

1. M.T. Beliavskii, *Krest'ianskii vopros*, p.292.
2. *Ibid.*, pp. 283-5.
3. P. Dukes, *Catherine the Great*, p.93.
4. *Ibid.*, pp.95-6.

On the serf condition of the peasants in Russia.

An investigation of the problem set by the Free Economic Society: "What is more useful for society, that the peasant should possess land as property, or only movable property, and how far must his rights to this or that possession extend?"

Before we start our discussion of the proposed question, for a better arrangement it is absolutely necessary to know, what we understand by the word *peasant*. Peasant in general means a man, who lives permanently in the country, assigned to and occupied by agriculture and whatever is connected with it, irrespective of the authority to which he is subject.

The division of the peasants.

Our peasants are divided into different types, according to: 1) Who they belong to, and thus they are called state, court, seigneurial. 2) Who is charged with the obligation — the man, or the land, to which both serfs and freemen belong. 3) Whether or not they have land, as a result of which they are called farmers or labourers.

Many other divisions of the peasantry are used by foreigners, but since they are unknown in Russia, they have no place here; because the situation of our peasants, excluding the Ukrainian, is all the same, and they are generally unfree in themselves and in their property. And so, leaving those aside, we consider it most necessary to examine, how much the slavery, to which our peasantry is subjected as far as property is concerned, can be harmful or useful.

The advantages of property.

Everyday experience shows us that personal advantage constitutes the chief object, on which all our thoughts tend to be centred, and which also encourages us to put up with all kinds of troubles; and what it represents in different aspects, this depends on the case and the upbringing. This can clearly be seen by recognising that by an inborn inclination we are continually concerned for our own happiness: *to seek that, which brings us actual satisfaction, and to avoid everything, which is inimical to it, are the two inexhaustible sources of virtue and sin.* It is necessary to know the best ways of turning these desires to the good, and to encourage them in a skilful manner: the consequences will definitely correspond to the intentions.

The peasant, whose ideas correspond to his condition, will in like manner endeavour to the extent of his strength and knowledge to increase his happiness, if he does not find in his undertakings such obstacles as sometimes force him against his will to be careless about himself. I think and not without reason, that possession of movable and immovable property can be considered as the sole and moreover by no means a bad way of encouraging and restoring the peasantry, which is however deprived of all the benefits and advantages connected with the rights of society; because a peasant, being lord of his own estate, not afraid of suffering coercion from any quarter, and using what he has obtained freely, may dispose of it and use it to his own benefit. He knows what he must do for the satisfaction of domestic needs or for the acquisition of a surplus; consequently he enthusiastically tries to find all possible ways of turning each opportunity to his advantage; marshy, sandy and hilly places will not tire his zealous hands, but everything must yield to his industry and bring benefit with a surplus. The members of his household will either voluntarily follow his example or carry out their tasks in the proper way because of strict supervision; nothing will be able to escape his attention, he will see everything; the smallest fault will upset him until he corrects it.

These benefits will also be conducive to a situation where, seeing some income accruing to himself, and priding himself on it, the peasant will spare nothing that serves the preservation of his health, and as well as clothing himself suitably for defence against the weather, may eat healthy food, which considerably helps the continuance of life and the spread of population; moreover in time of serious illness he will be in a better position to regain his health than a have-not. As far as the spread of the human race is concerned, a prosperous peasant, always knowing that his children during his lifetime and at his death will not suffer a distressed situation, is always delighted by the increase of his family, and, according to his circumstances, the peasant attempts to give them a proper upbringing.

From this it also follows, that besides an exact return of poll-tax and quitrent, the petty bourgeoisie must equally expect no small profit: because beyond the cheapness of necessary comestibles, as a result of peasant diligence, there will be an abundance of worthwhile goods, such as, for example: hemp, flax, wool, hides, etc., which, being processed in factories, will serve towards the eradication of idleness among the people and the feeding of many thousands. Finally, from a peasantry possessing its own property the whole state will feel great relief: its earnings will grow incomparably, and in case of necessity, apart from the reserves, strong support can be expected from them.

Let us take on the other hand the man possessing no freedom in property, let us consider his spiritual and bodily qualities. This sad object appears before my eyes as nothing more than the living image of idleness, negligence, distrust and fear; in a word he bears on his face all the hallmarks of a disastrous life and an oppressive misfortune.

To reason justly, from a humanity deprived of all rights and a man brought to the ultimate despondency, nothing better can be expected.

We cannot demand that a man sunk so low should strive in the proper way; because he knows in advance, that from his labours nothing will come but danger, torture and oppression. His sole concern, and that enforced, consists of somehow satisfying basic needs, and so he spends all his time in idleness, considering it an alleviation of his wretchedness. In spite of his distressing situation, nothing concerns him; emulation, endeavour and thoughts about the correction of his situation are completely unknown to him. He is always badly dressed, eats bad food, takes no interest in family affairs, the increase of the family is a burden to him, in a word, everything about which another would be infinitely pleased, brings him great sorrow. Therefore, their life is short, the spread of the human race thus meets with great obstacles, their upbringing leads not to the correction, but to the greater corruption of their morals, and society not only cannot place its hopes on them or receive any assistance in case of need; but on the contrary they are always a burden to it and demand from it continual aid.

Not without reason many renowned people assert that extreme oppression is not only harmful for society, but also dangerous. Not to mention the Romans, the Lacedaemonians and others, peoples which suffered great harm and ruin from their own slaves, our neighbour Poland in recent times, on the occasion of Cossack revolts, has seen the arms of its oppressed peasants turned against itself, and has been greatly shaken. The helots, suffering under the yoke of unbearable slavery, strongly shook the Lacedaemonian republic; the Romans brought the slave war to an end with great harm to themselves, and saw Sicily, their best province, brought by the slaves into ruins. Similarly our neighbour Poland suffered great losses from the oppressed peasants during the Cossack revolts. And indeed, a man possessing no benefits which would inspire him to the preservation of such a society, where he is nothing and is always suffering, must have little enthusiasm for it; he knows, that whatever change occurs in it, he has nothing to lose; sometimes it also happens, that such people, seeing no end to their misfortunes, despair completely and go to extremes dangerous for every society. So for the improvement of the depressed condition of such peasants, some sovereigns beneficially conceded them property rights, or made the manner of attaining freedom easier. So this and the other arrangement serve to their own glory and to the advantage of their whole fatherland.

On the origin of the slave condition.
In order to know, on what laws slavery stands confirmed and whence it arose, it is absolutely necessary to seek its beginnings in the most remote past, and we shall see later to our great astonishment, that the origin of the peasantry, the lowest of all, but the most necessary,

class in every society, must be ascribed to force.

Of this nobody will have any doubt, that natural law, instilled in our hearts by the Creator Himself, for our perfection, does not contain the reason for such an institution; that people should agree to it voluntarily and subject themselves to such a cruel sacrifice, can also not be believed, reasoning particularly by the inclination inborn in man towards the acquisition of happiness and by the insuperable striving for freedom. And so another reason for it of which we can be completely convinced must be sought.

With many others, I think that this must be ascribed to war, which not only, for the time that it continues, brings about very sad operations, but even at its conclusion leaves the clearest marks of its cruelty; war, I say, is the reason for the most wretched condition, in which so many similar to us suffer. Ancient peoples, as is evident from the history of all ages, considered it a general law to bring prisoners into a slave condition, attributing to themselves moreover, perhaps for their own greater security and benefit, the full authority of life and death over such men; and this opinion, as can clearly be seen from Roman laws, spread so far that, excluding them from the number of people, they assigned them to things. The Romans and the Greeks, so famous, so enlightened before all other peoples, can serve as an excellent example of the confirmation of this truth, and we find in their chronicles, that whole peoples were subjected to this misfortune: the helots of the Lacedaemonians, the peons of the Thessalonians, by the laws of war at that time, constituted a peasant condition, subjected to unbearable miseries. The Romans, at unbroken war for several centuries running, and behaving with prisoners according to the practice of these times, collected a terrible multitude of these unfortunates, who, with the corruption of morals in the Roman republic, served to the satisfaction of luxury and pride, and were tortured in an inhuman way. The composition of these republics did not allow the free man to occupy himself with crafts and commerce, which were held by them in great contempt; on the other hand, everything that made them capable of carrying on all warlike tasks, was rated very highly. In such a way, prisoners taken into captivity, like our servants although with dissimilar profit, had to carry on all kinds of work in the homes of their lords and outside them. Doctors, all kinds of craftsmen, merchants, farmers were from this order of people, and the cruelty of their sacrifice in Europe did not change with the affirmation of the Christian faith. A similar example, although with a different severity, we find with the Franks or Frenchmen as they are now who, after the conquest of Gaul, relying on the superiority of their forces, enslaved the natives. The Burgundians, the Goths acted likewise in the lands that they conquered. They were not the first to carry on this practice, but brought it with them from Germany, their common fatherland, where, according to the testimony of Tacitus, it was widely used; of which several remains are even now to be seen in the German land.

The founders of Russia, after the example of other peoples, were of the same opinion, and the military order, being then dominant, turned the thoughts of all upon itself. For this reason, all arts and crafts were very much neglected, so that in the time of the first grand dukes, not only weapons, but even clothes had to be obtained by war as the following speech of Igor's retinue clearly shows: "The followers of Sveinald are equipped with weapons and fine clothes, but we are naked. So let us go to gather tribute, Prince, and you will gain and so will we", and so on. Almost ceaseless wars and expeditions, it can readily be concluded, demanded a great number of people, particularly for those times, and gave little time for thought and endeavour in domestic affairs. And so, to compensate for the drawbacks of frequent absence, some kind of advantageous means had to be found, which would correspond equally to the drawback. The selfsame wars gave quite a good opportunity for this, since they collected a great number of prisoners, who, by ancient custom, were brought into slavery and included with other plunder. For, in spite of the simplicity that there was then, the citizen had his house, his family, his land and fields, so he could not do without people who occupied themselves exclusively with household management. This business was entrusted to prisoners, whom they used as servants in town, and for agriculture outside it. We find a memorable passage in the Kievan Chronicle, serving very well as a confirmation of this truth, where the author speaks about the conquest by Saint Olga of the Derevlian land in the following manner, that she "killed some, and gave others to her followers as slaves; and she spared the rest to pay tribute, and levied a heavy tribute on them". However, that this order of people was already known in Russia, we have not the slightest reason to doubt. The words *cheliadin* and *smerd*, which so frequently occur in our old chronicles and laws, bear very clear witness to this, nothing else but the slave status, with the sole difference of expression that *cheliadin* means domestic servant, and *smerd* farmer or peasant. Ancient laws of the Russian people also clearly point out this difference, as we see from these words of Iaroslav's laws: "And shall a slave strike a free man?"

It must not be forgotten, that the number of these unfortunate people greatly increased through a voluntary, and sometimes enforced, crime: because daily experience shows us that many, although by nature free, thinking of finishing their wretchedness and hoping to seek a defence for themselves, have preferred slave status to high-born freedom and disgraced themselves forever, and made their descendants miserable.

The wretched condition of our peasants.

This harsh and inhuman law of war was preserved in its entirety right up to our times, and we see quite well the effects of this experience on our peasantry, whose impoverished condition has gone to such an extreme degree that, deprived of almost all human qualities so to speak, they cannot see the size of their misfortune and seem to be weighed down by a permanent slumber.

Peasants justly deserve all possible care, and neither time nor labour should be spared to bring them into good circumstances. To speak the truth, so many must be obliged to such people who, being always ready for the defence of the fatherland, spill their blood for it, who, saving others arduous tasks and worries, feed them abundantly, who having themselves almost nothing, provide others so generously, who, not having any enjoyment themselves throughout their whole lives, are exclusively occupied with the increase of the benefit of others: in a word, our life, our security, all our advantages are in their power and coupled in an indestructible union with their condition. But we, if we confess sincerely, forgetting all these great benefactions, pay with scorn instead of honour, render insults instead of thanks, instead of concern nothing is visible but ruination.

Nothing can bring a man into greater dejection, than to deprive him of human rights. Because of this we gradually become negligent and lazy, which depresses us and imperceptibly takes away our strength and impedes our intellect from rising to the appropriate level of fulfilment. Having gone that far, perpetual distrust and a certain fear do not allow us to penetrate the thick clouds of ignorance. But let a man have human rights, let all obstacles not allowing him to carry them into effect be destroyed, then his strength will return and he will soon become a new man.

With their sad example, our peasants can show how disastrous for people is extreme oppression. And so above all, it is necessary to realise that for the glory of the people and the benefit of society the dishonourable trade carried on in human blood must be abolished. In this case, not making any distinction between inanimate objects and man, we sell our neighbours like pieces of wood and pity our cattle more than people. This must be completely eradicated, and irrespective of the reasons in favour of it that somebody may put forward. It is enough that the welfare of the society demands it, and in fact the advantage of a small number of people, if it can be called an advantage, when it tends towards their own ruin, cannot be brought into consideration. I do not mean here the final prohibition; but whoever wants to sell, must sell everything together, land and people, and not separate parents from children, brothers from sisters, friends from friends; because, not to mention other disparities, from this piecemeal sale the people will die out, and agriculture suffer terrible decline.

I cannot find such poor people as our peasants, who, having no defence from the laws, are subject to all possible wrongs in respect not only of property, but even of life itself, and suffer boundless effrontery, torture and oppression; from which inevitably they must sink down into that condition, full of woes for themselves and society, in which we now see them. And so, without further discussion of these poor people, everybody can easily conclude this from the reduced state of their existence, actions and thoughts, which appear to us as nothing but a very lamentable spectacle; but leaving these sad pitiable objects, let us turn to the matter itself.

Having briefly considered the various kinds of peasantry, the use of property and the harm of its non-possession, the origin of the slave status and the poverty of our peasants, the means of its reform must be considered, and so for better order we divide them into four parts, from which

1) We will talk about the institution of peasant education.

2) About the assignment to the peasants of property in land with appropriate limitations, and about the grant to them of full control over movable property and other benefits.

3) About the establishment of separate courts for the defence of the peasants.

4) About precautions with this reform.

On the institution of peasant education.

The aforementioned neglect of public education, unpardonable in our own times, is the cause of great calamities; and it is so well known that there is so little thought about it that we still have no arrangements which could be used advantageously in the general improvement of morals. The most important matter on which the general welfare depends, and with which it is linked by an inseparable bond, is never unfortunately given a thought. It seems to me, *that to enlighten people with teaching, to preserve their health by the inculcation of diligence and by physical exercises, to set them on the path of a virtuous life with the help of a healthy moral training*, must be the principal objects of the laws, and their greatest endeavour must be to this end. On consideration, it is obvious from all the evidence, that we are very far away from this; the impatience or short-sightedness of some, the ignorance or self-interest of others, not to mention many reasons similar to them, are an insuperable obstacle to the completion of this great business.

It seems almost incredible, how much education contributes to the welfare of every society, and for that reason it must occupy the first place here. Everybody knows to what great vices the common people is usually subject: ignorance, superstition, intemperance, idleness, thoughtlessness make us not only contemptuous of it, but sometimes hate it. The best way, some think, of holding back its violent folly, is severity, force and executions, not thinking that this might lead to the aggravation rather than to the cure of the wounds. Other ways may be found of serving to the achievement of this intention with better advantage. I mean education, with the help of which, as experience has many times shown us, every man, of no matter what status, can be reformed. As far as the peasants, of whom we must talk here particularly, are concerned, it is definitely necessary in their case to take such measures as correspond to the simplicity of their life and status; so, we suggest how, starting from infancy, they should be treated at this tender age.

In each village, where circumstances allow, schools should be set up for the teaching of Russian reading and writing, at least reading, and the first foundations of faith, to young peasant children. From the small villages, where this cannot be done, peasants must send their children to the nearest schools for instruction, unless some impossibility stops them: then it remains for them to follow the example of others.

Each peasant must send his ten-year-old children to school in wintertime, so that they will have learned in good time what is necessary for their status, and will not have any obstacles at work after their maturity.

The necessary books must be given to them free in the first instance. For this purpose a primer must be compiled, with church and civil script, also the former Russian and presently used figures, and appended to it a simple catechism. The ten commandments given by God to Moses can serve as a basis; a sensible explanation of them is very necessary; besides this it must include the first foundations of Evangelical teaching, briefly, clearly and without any admixture of subtleties. These books, for the relief of peasant wretchedness, must be sold at the lowest price and be thoroughly prepared. The county consistories can look after them and send them out promptly as they are asked for by the priests who, having sold them with the price listed on the first page for the avoidance of all deceit, will bring the money to the consistory. Church readers can occupy the position of teachers in the schools, and they must teach the beginners reading and writing, and teach those who know these to learn the catechism by heart. They must also hand out certificates of baptism printed in the priest's hand so that nobody can conceal his age;[1] because it is very useful to indicate the number, age and property of the members constituting society.

For each church and school one priest and reader should be enough, in which, besides the execution of their duties, they must observe a sinless way of life. The example of such a person can make a greater impression than elevated arguments surpassing the understanding of simple people. Moreover such people should be selected as priests and readers who know something of household management; since, seeing good usage, the peasant can understand it better than words or force. Beyond a proper execution of God's service, the priest must teach the peasants in church the Word of God, eradicate from them superstition, inculcate respect, love and fidelity to the sovereign, appeal to their conscience for a virtuous way of life and work; moreover, as much as possible, simply, with seemly brevity and directly. He must also read in this assembly for three Sundays running, decrees published about the peasants or in some way concerning them, carry on a strict supervision over the school, set right great inadequacies, examine the peasant children in their studies, and interpret the catechism to them in church on Sundays and holidays.

Such people must be distinguished by enough honour and subsistence, and have before them the hope of receiving a decent reward for their labours. To this end, the priest and the reader must depend exclusively on the bishop and the county consistory, which to empty places must send others on demand, and exchange and punish the unworthy, according to their own inspection or sound complaints; all must be forbidden to take anything on the side at their own volition, and there must be no weakening in this.

For honourable subsistence, the priest and the reader should be given enough land and a suitable house with everything necessary for household management. The consistory must concern itself with the house and all its requirements, and a noble or his steward with the allotment of the land. Beyond this, they must be afforded a regular income from christenings, weddings, funerals, etc., so that there shall be no burden for the peasant, nor shame for the priest. But so that their labour and concern should not be without charity, in recognition of the industriousness and goodness of such virtuous churchpeople, for their greater encouragement they can be transferred from the country to the towns, and assigned to good parishes. But so that this should not remain without effect, send out annually from the most holy governing Synod learned spiritual personages as inspectors. The governing senate, for greater correctness, can attach to the spiritual people skilled laymen, who must try with all their strength to stamp out irregularities. These supervisors must not at all depend on each other, but at the end of the business entrusted them, each must give detailed and accurate information to the office in which he has his position.

All this is proposed here as briefly as possible. The spiritual court, with the addition of secular learned and skilled people, can add much in connection with the duties of the priest and reader, their strict supervision by each county consistory, and their decent subsistence. It is also necessary to furnish the churchmen with good direction for their task and conduct.

Physical strength is more necessary to the peasants than to others, so for the preservation of health apothecaries must be appointed to large villages, and they should maintain for their better subsistence a pharmacy, with the absolutely necessary medicines moderate in price and number according to the simple peasant situation. I would want these apothecaries to occupy themselves with curing cattle, which after all would bring great benefit to household management. The College of Medicine can give a full recommendation for this and with strict supervision oblige the apothecaries to observe their duties exactly. There can be no thought about the appointment of skilled and trained midwives, although this would be very useful, because they cannot be found not only in the villages, but even in the towns. In time, there must be considered the appointment to the villages of doctors, and each must be assigned an area with a sufficient number of villages; because, not to mention that they can help more in dangerous cases than an apothecary, they can also apply themselves to the discovery of much information about flora, animals and fish, and thus be of great help to natural history.

The police can justly be called the unshakable support of the people's security; for this it is necessary to set it up and keep it up with full force, not only in the towns but also in the villages. The expenses incurred will be repaid a hundredfold, and what seems very difficult at first will later seem a mere trifle.

The duties of police officials in the villages must consist of the good supervision of roads, forcing peasants in their time to repair them, or to clear new ones, the eradication of thieves and brigands, help with advice and action in case of fire, and for such an end arranging in each village for inexpensive firehoses and other useful implements, the supervision of building, and care that there is cleanliness and tidiness in the villages, as much as circumstances allow. They must also conserve the forest, and where necessity demands cut it for building or firewood, then ordering young trees to be planted in those places and to watch over them with proper care, not allowing rivers and lakes to dry up, particularly those along which boats may want to go.

The difficulty is to find capable and industrious people, and because of this we see for the most part, that the best institutions not only remain inactive, but sometimes, because of their bad operation or complete neglect, are the reason for trouble among the people. There must be much thought about this, and mental and physical resources must be carefully found. But rather than there being distrust in this case, for greater efficiency the rural police must be subjected to that of the town, to which the rural police officials must give an account every year. After this the town police will send trusted people for eye-witness inspection.

On the ownership of immovable property.

In a suggestion of ways of improving peasant upbringing, it needs to be asked what property should the peasant possess and within what limits should his rights over it be confined, so that this should tend towards not only the personal advantage of the peasant, but of all those who must participate in the change, and each person possess what justly should belong to him.

It is not necessary to take examples from others here, but it must be exclusively based on good sense and on the rules of the love of mankind, never losing sight moreover of the general welfare. Each state has its own peculiar composition, faults and excellences; and so it should almost never happen, that the laws and institutions of one state could be profitably applied to another. The introduction of Roman laws into many European powers is almost a monstrosity, and we hear daily complaints; however, because it is known for what reason they have been introduced and retained, we shall hear the same complaints henceforth.

Reasoning by the assignment of the peasants, we may easily see why we possess them; and so as a consequence of this each peasant must have enough land for the sowing of corn and the pasturage of cattle, and possess it in an hereditary manner, so that the landlord will not have the least authority to oppress him in any way, or even to take it away completely, i.e. while the peasant properly observes all his duties; because otherwise he can be deprived of these benefits as a punishment for being unworthy, and they can be granted to another. However, before the landlord can do this, the case must be examined in the appropriate court.

The hereditary right to lands must not extend as far as the irrevocable damage and great ruin of the proprietors, so that the peasant would be in a position to dispose at will of the property given him by another; it is enough, if he can use it without let or hindrance and get subsistence from it. For this reason, he should not be permitted, no matter on what pretext he wants to do it, to sell his land, give it away, mortgage it or divide it among his children, but at the death of the father one of his sons will become the owner; thus the proprietor will always have his rights and the peasant will freely use the benefits afforded him.

Since it may happen, that with the increase of families there will not be enough land for subsistence in a village, the appropriate measure must be immediately taken in such an instance; as far as the court peasants are concerned no such deficiency must be feared; but as it will soon be noticed that the land cannot feed them, so, to avert this wretched deficiency forever, several families must be taken immediately from their former area and settled in an empty area, but families must not be separated and single people must not be taken alone. For this purpose, each county court must know, how many areas there are under their jurisdiction empty and suitable for agriculture, have implements appropriate to agriculture in readiness, provide settlers with seeds, cattle and in case of need, give them money for all this without repayment. Good homes for them must also be built, and in the first instance they should be freed from all impositions for several years, depending on the quality of the soil, so that they can have enough time to set themselves straight. Nobles who do not have enough land must buy according to the suitability of the area, and if there are not enough such opportunities, then peasants can be allowed away (the reason written in their passports) to work in factories, or what is even better, to set them learning trades with which they can make a living even in the country.

Agriculture demands many people, and the encouragement of marriage is absolutely necessary in this case. For this the simplest means can be devised, for example, allowing married people to have precedence before the single, freeing those who have many children from some of the burdens imposed upon them, etc. It must also be taken into consideration, that the presence of rural inhabitants in the towns can very much harm agriculture; because from whatever the citizen has for his worthy subsistence the peasant takes some, and meanwhile agriculture, the most necessary, the most profitable wealth for each society, will be extremely neglected, not to mention that the peasants are often spoiled by urban licence and luxury, become accustomed to idleness and make themselves incapable of carrying out rural tasks; therefore there should be the strongest attempt to keep them from this and to force them to live according to their assignment.

I know that we do not have a middle class, and to banish peasants from the towns might occasion great shortages; therefore such an important change cannot be brought into society without difficulty; however, if we think in the proper way, we will soon find people suitable for it.[2] A wise sovereign, an enlightened minister, will quickly find a way of overcoming the obstacles that they meet; only weak souls in the perpetual gloom of ignorance, reasoning by the small size of their world, consider it impossible with the eradication of old-fashioned prejudices to open for themselves a clear path. A great spirit, lifting itself above the others, views with an ambitious eye the whole connection of the social structure, and discovering without difficulty the basis, growth and completion of phenomena in the ethical world, has enough strength for the cessation, or diversion, or increase of their flow and speed.

On the ownership of movable property.

This is not enough for the defence of these poor people: the property acquired by their labour must not be brought into jeopardy. All peasant wealth consists of agriculture and cattle, and this may be called their own trade, from which exclusively they must derive their living, and from the profit accruing from it they must share out part to the sovereign and to the lord, and at the same time be content.

As far as movable property is concerned, consisting of cattle and the fruits of agriculture, I think, that in respect of this the peasants should be given full authority and freedom. Let us assume, that at first they receive all these things from the bounty of others, and thus get into a position to give themselves and their family enough sustenance; from this it does not follow however that their benefactors can ascribe to themselves full rights over the property acquired by their labour because of this bounty, which is also very burdensome; it is enough, if the peasant pays his lord a certain share annually as a mark of his gratitude, and this would infinitely exceed what had been given him; and so in the end not the peasant but the lord will be the debtor and consequently in case of misfortune he will be obliged to help the peasant. Beyond these reasons, the general welfare must be taken into consideration, and this demands that every member of society, carrying out in the proper manner the duty assigned him, may freely use the benefits obtained by his labours, and, in case of the violent or surreptitious destruction of them, justice must defend them. On the other hand, if full authority over any kind of property is left to the lord, then the peasantry can never raise itself; the danger of his final ruin will prohibit him from seeking help in court, and, serving as a sacrifice to incessant persecutions and tortures, he will always be in low spirits.

Moreover, it is absolutely necessary to assign other trades to the peasants, so that these trades, always having a certain connection with agriculture, will not distract them from it, but solely so that the peasants with their help might supply themselves and other. For this, certain days may be appointed, for example each Sunday, on which peasants with their help might supply themselves and others. For this, always very capably supply the towns, and bring for sale all kinds of grain, hemp, flax, cloth, cheese, butter, vegetables and many other things contributing to necessary human sustenance, and in this there should be no interference or encumbrance, but all possible assistance. To remain in the towns, and to carry on there trades not compatible with their status and calling may be forbidden them, and they should not be given any concession at all on this point.

Prescription of regular services and payments to the sovereign and to the lord.

When they are brought into such a reasonable status and allowed such great benefits, justice itself demands that they should in proportion give equal gratitude, carrying out with enthusiasm and energy the obligations placed upon them for the sovereign and the lord.

As regards the taxes, it is necessary to act with great prudence. The greatest difficulty consists of the fact that they cannot be exactly defined so that they would be equal, when the different position of countries and the consequent unequal income from property in them are taken into consideration; because of this, the best way of arranging taxes in my opinion is the establishment of the tithe or other part of all the fruits of agriculture. As regards money payment in general, it may be said that the more fully the people are enriched, the more taxes can be collected from them, and if we look for an actual income between the tax and the people's wealth, then they are just, and nobody can complain. The services demanded from the peasants on behalf of the lord may be arranged in the following manner, that the peasant may work for his lord one day, and the others for himself.

The prescription of regular taxes for the cessation of robbery and ruin is absolutely necessary; because such an arrangement will defend the peasants more than a little from the contempt of their landlords, who torture them without any mercy or charity, taking away from them everything that comes before their eyes, and bringing them into untold misery, from which they are never in a position to save themselves.

In time of flood, cattle plague, poor harvest and other great misfortunes, to restore the peasants it is absolutely necessary to help them with money or remission of taxes for a certain time, the arrears of which they can repay after their recovery.

The nobility will suffer no harm from the limitation of its arbitrariness, and although at first glance it will appear that the loss of property and the prescription of regular services and taxes destroys the major part of their rights over the peasants; however, taking into consideration other circumstances and throwing all harmful prejudices aside, everybody then may easily see that this is not only not bad for them but more advantageous than previously, and society will feel no small relief. However, they will always keep enough rights, such as for example, hunting, fishing, authority over their woods, which solely for the benefit of society as a whole should be limited to a certain extent; and after all, according to the practice of foreign nobility, they may be allowed to administer a civil court for their peasants, about which we will now speak.

On the institution of peasant courts.

It may very easily happen, that the lords, in contempt for their peasants and in expectation of the advantages of their status, will oppress them and occasion them all kinds of injuries; it is therefore absolutely necessary to give them security, as a result of a justice based upon a secure foundation, with the help of which they may defend themselves against all kinds of unjust attacks and oppressions.

Insults may be occasioned a peasant either by a peasant or by the lord. These cases should be dealt with in such a way that, according to the importance of the insult, the proper courts may be set up, so that there should not be superfluous red-tape and expenses. To such an end, they should choose an elder from among themselves, and, assigning to him three or four men, present them to their lord for approval.

These rural judges[3] must decide the most minor cases, such as verbal insults, quarrels, small lawsuits, etc. And as far as important arguments among themselves or with their lords are concerned, superior peasant courts[4] should be instituted for this under the supervision of people who undoubtedly possess knowledge and skill in the exercise of the Russian laws, and empower them to examine and decide important cases of dispute between the peasants and the lords. In case of dissatisfaction and unjust decision, for appeal to rural courts let there be high-rank nobles, to whom for greater correctness and order assign people knowing the law, who must only on demand give their opinion and advice, so that nothing tending to the destruction of the law can happen, but everything be done as justice requires. All this is concerned with civil courts, because criminal affairs do not pertain to these courts.

The precautions to be taken with this reform.

It now remains to say, what precautions must be taken with such an important reform. It is known that this cannot be brought into effect immediately without great danger, and it is already confirmed by many examples how far the fury of the common people stretches in such cases; and so it is useful to take measures, which, while not destroying the general peace, could show clearly to all that these decisions are conducive to their own welfare.

Before it is possible to commence this reform, I consider it necessary to prepare the peasants in advance through education, carried on under the direction of good churchpeople; when this had been done with sufficient precision, first of all, as an example to the nobility, court and state peasants should be selected, from whom only zealous and good peasants should be rewarded with these benefits and the lazy and bad not allowed these advantages; but, allowing time for their improvement, exhort them in all possible ways to turn away from their bad life and for their greater encouragement, present them these benefits, if only they will correct themselves.

On confirmation of this great institution, the more to encourage them to diligence, rich peasants may be allowed to join the petty bourgeoisie, not simply but with several contracts, so that the final emptying of the villages can be averted. Thus watch closely if such a peasant is in a position to buy himself a house in town; if he has enough money for his commitments, and can pay the sovereign or the lord the levy on each soul that he brings with him from the village. If he has money for all this, then he may be allowed to change his residence and status.

The nobility, whom this business concerns particularly, should not be forced at all; because each of them, when convinced of his own advantage, will agree with good will to introduce such institutions, which, occasioning him not the smallest harm, will serve to the welfare of those people, for the conservation of whom, love of humanity and his own benefit will oblige him to put forward every effort.

I shall be obliged to consider myself not otherwise than completely happy, if this my labour corresponds to the demands of those who occasioned this suggestion. However, I make bold to affirm, that all my wishes are to serve my fatherland; I have exclusively undertaken this work with such a resolve and sincerely desire that, under the blessed power of our Great Sovereign, Russia will peacefully enjoy the prosperity being prepared under her wise direction, bringing heartfelt thanks to the Most-High Creator for the great bounty that He pours out.

Polenov's Footnotes

1. Specimen certificate. To the peasant X was born a son or daughter at 2 o'clock in the afternoon of 9 November 1767. The child was christened on 12 November 1767 and at the christening the name X was given, as was witnessed by the priest X.
2. We have in the towns many tradespeople on state income. If we free all these people and give them some help in the first instance, we may create a numerous petty bourgeoisie, and if we give them the proper liberties, according to the example of other European peoples, we will encourage their diligence. Other peoples, judging according to the quality of their lands, should be our inferior in many respects; however, in spite of that, we see that they are superior to us in almost every way: out of nothing, so to speak, they are performing miracles. Having made arrangements in the manner suggested, we will quickly see the same: the towns will be populated with worthy inhabitants useful for society, their beauty will be enhanced by magnificent buildings; the state income will grow incomparably; sciences, crafts and commerce will be in blooming condition, and everybody will then consider himself happy, not being the slightest burden to society.
3. It is an urgent need, because of the simplicity and ignorance of the peasants, to compose a brief set of regulations, which will contain in it everything pertaining to their duty, and describe in detail which cases come within their

competence, and which punishment they must prescribe for the guilty.

4. These superior courts must also be given good instructions, so that the rich will not be favoured over the poor, nor the strong over the weak, but everybody will receive an adequate recompense according to his deserts.

From *Russkii arkhiv*, 1865.

7. P.I. Rychkov's Instructions for a Steward or Bailiff, 1770

INTRODUCTION

Peter Ivanovich Rychkov was born into a merchant's family in 1712, and himself entered business at an early age. After learning modern methods of accountancy and transferring to government service, he was sent at the age of twenty-two to be book-keeper for the administration of the frontier territory of Orenburg. There, his interests widened, and he became an expert on the history, geography and economy of the area at the same time as keeping its finances in order. He produced many publications, became the first corresponding member of the Academy of Sciences, and had risen sufficiently high in the Table of Ranks by the time of the convocation of the Legislative Assembly to offer his candidature as deputy for the Orenburg nobility, albeit unsuccessfully. He continued to devote much of his attention to aspects of life in Orenburg, including bare survival at the time of the Pugachev Revolt, until his death in 1777.

Rychkov was an early and enthusiastic member of the Free Economic Society, and submitted papers to it on a wide range of topics, including the products to be obtained from cotton and camel hair, the conservation and increase of forests and methods of expanding agriculture in Orenburg Province. The contribution to the Free Economic Society's *Works* which has been chosen for translation here was in the first instance, like Polenov's essay, an entry for a competition. Absence of the lord from his estate, through either the calls of service or the lure of the big cities was a common phenomenon in and around the year 1770, when Rychkov's *Instruction* was published. While Rychkov shares the enthusiasm of his enlightened contemporaries for education and for technological innovation, as well as their belief in the pre-eminence of agriculture, he is closer to the soil in practice than most of them, and writes from experience as well as from reading. Although written to help the steward or bailiff, the *Instruction* also acquaints us with the day-to-day concerns of the majority of his fellow-countrymen. It is an obvious enough point, but one too often forgotten, that problems such as damp and mice in grain stooks bothered many more inhabitants of the Russian Empire than did those of philosophy.

A wider setting for Rychkov's observations may be obtained through the views of others made in different parts of the Russian Empire. For example, describing the situation in the Kashira district of the central Moscow Province, A.T. Bolotov wrote that the worst hindrance to the progress of agriculture was the confused division of the fields. The peasant never worked consolidated land adjacent to his cottage and vegetable patch; always he had to struggle with strips scattered around all the fields attached to the local village. The lands of the proprietor might be together, but many villages would be divided among several proprietors, and there would be boundary disputes between them, and much bickering concerning the use made of meadows, woods and other appendages held in common. Even when harmony reigned, it was impossible for peasants to plough or manure the land properly, and none of them could do all his sowing at the most favourable time. Crops under cultivation could not be looked after in the proper manner, nor could incursions of animals be prevented at growing or harvest time. Yet, for all the failure of his efforts to persuade his fellow local proprietors to agree on some joint action to clear up the mess, Bolotov was optimistic about the progress of agriculture in his district.

Evidence provided by Bolotov himself and by other contributors to the *Works* of the Free Economic Society lent little foundation to such optimism. For example, the Society was interested in the introduction of new crops such as potatoes and wheat, but replies to a questionnaire revealed that wheat was not cultivated very much and that potatoes had not even been heard of in some regions. The belief was strong that the three-field system of agriculture was the best, but resistance to it was reported from some districts, such as Vologda in Archangel Province, and elsewhere, for example in new lands to the south, the approach to agriculture was persistently extensive.

While there were few grounds for optimism as far as progress in agriculture in the late eighteenth century was concerned, the assertion that there was no change at all would be equally invalid. The area under cultivation was certainly expanding, and farming in general was making a response to increased market demands. Soviet historians have clearly indicated the social adjustments accompanying this response, in particular the stratification of the peasantry, which was already beginning to undermine the institution of serfdom. Spokesmen for the nobility were reluctant to recognise the implications for the landlords of an economic upsurge affecting country as well as town and factory. Indeed, such writers as Rychkov devoted their energies to working out ways in which prosperity would occur without any alteration to the basic social structure of rural Russia.

Here are the equivalents of the measurements to be found below, particularly in points 4, 6, 13, 16, 18 and 21:

arshin	– 712mm or 28ins.
dessiatine	– 1.0925 hectares or 2.7 acres.
pood	– 16.38kg or 36 lbs.

quarter	— *either* 2.099 hectolitres or 6 bushels.
	or a quarter sagene.
sagene (sazhen)	— 2.134 metres or 7 feet.

Instructions for a steward or bailiff, about the good maintenance and management of villages in the absence of the lord.

Each steward or bailiff, starting to run the farms and villages entrusted to him, must first become fully acquainted with his lord's rights, both to the land with all the appurtenances and to the people and peasants who belong to those estates; and particularly everything that concerns the lands and all rural appurtenances. If he starts his duties in summer, and not winter time; then, not delaying it until after other matters, taking with him old residents from the best houses, and some middle-aged and young people, he should go around all the cottages, and find out from these rural inhabitants, how far on each side the boundaries and limits stretch, and where whatever adjacant lands there are finish. If the estates entrusted to him do not have a plan, he should ask for one from the lord, and when the lord does not have one; then he may try to make some kind of a drawing, showing on it rivers, natural limits and other boundaries according to the deeds, so that everything may be seen at a glance, and clearly recollected, for the quickest explanation and solution of all arguments arising. And write down the names of whoever is with him on such an inspection, and keep them with the affairs of the estate, so that in the case of change of steward or bailiff afterwards, they can be used for such an inspection, and there will always be people who know the limits and boundaries. Similarly, as far as the people are concerned, try to find out who was attached to which lord of that estate; because even in one village there are living people belonging to the landlords by different registers, consequently such information about them is not unuseful to new bailiffs and stewards. Particularly in cases when they run away or are off in service.

2

The first point above must be observed not only on large farms and estates by stewards and bailiffs; but also in small villages by elders and elected officials, even by all the peasants, for their peaceful existence; but this second point is no less necessary for the enlightenment and prosperity of our rural inhabitants, and I make reference to it before other Economic affairs: it is known, that we have not only small, but even particularly large villages, where there is not one person able to read and write. On this point nearly all peoples inhabiting Europe and observing the Christian law are superior to us. Even the Tartars observing the Mohammedan law and living in the Empire disgrace us in this. As far as I know, there is almost not one of their villages, where there are not schools for the reading of the necessary prayers by young children, both male and female sexes being taught, with the sole difference, that the boys and girls of poor fathers rarely learn to write. From our peasants' lack of education, there is so much ignorance, coarseness, unsuitability and extremely bad conduct, that, as of a well-known fact, I consider it superfluous to expatiate on them here. The infant children of our peasants lounge about the villages from eight years of age and further, and become accustomed exclusively to inactivity and idleness, from which, at their maturity, great harm is done to them and the state. To eradicate this, it is very needful and necessary that the stewards and bailiffs on each farm and in each village, keep at the very least one man knowing how to read and write, and, choosing from the best peasant children of the male sex from six to eight years, order them to learn reading and the most necessary prayers of the Christian duty, and teach those who turn out to be the most understanding and reliable how to write as well; however, only so much, that in a village of a hundred souls there should not be more than two or three persons knowing how to write; because it can be observed that there are some such people who have learned how to write who often use their knowledge for evil purposes, the composition of false passports, and the like; but there will be more who know how to read only, for their own enlightenment, and more usefully, for all society. Meanwhile a good steward or bailiff will not cease to be concerned about this, and to encourage the people and peasants subject to them, so that on Sundays and holidays, and particularly in Lent, they will carry out their Christian duties, on which their happiness and prosperity depend.[1]

3

He who takes over the running of villages from the former steward, or whoever it is, must demand an inventory of what at his arrival in the estate entrusted to him belongs to the lord, and specifically: he must have described the lord's house with the people of the lord's household, and with all its belongings, horses, all kinds of cattle, etc: if there are any, factories, works, mills or the like. He must also measure and describe the grain on hand of every kind, and the number of dessiatines in all three fields, how much is ploughed and sown with grain for the landlord, and how many household and labouring peasants there are in the estate entrusted to him, and he must inform the lord about the whole establishment, keeping for himself among the records of the estate the information that must be the primary basis and proof of how he found the estate and what entered his establishment. And after a year enter in a single list under each item what has been gained or lost, and what remains for the new year, and, making such inventories annually, send them to the landlord, from which the increase and decrease respectively and his concern for the rural Economy will always be apparent. He must particularly keep records of income and expenditure,[2] and use people for this and for household services by the special order of the lord. As far as monthly grain distribution to the people of the lord's household and other expenditures are concerned, similarly the money payments, which are levied on anybody at the will of the lord; keep a special register for these and use it to make sure that the sum levied on each person comes in on time; but meanwhile if unnecessary earlier monetary and grain outlays be discovered, inform the landlord about them with an explanation, and see that there is no unnecessary or superfluous expenditure on anything. I include this last point particularly because there are in the lords' houses of our countryside many parasites and useless expenditures, and from this an unnoticed but nevertheless great loss occurs to the property of the landlord.

4

The old practice in the farms and villages of the landlords (excluding those on quitrent) was to reckon the lord's arable land in dessiatines, and although according to the old manorial records they were measured 30 sagenes across and 80 along, and this is called by us a regular dessiatine, the landlords' dessiatines almost everywhere are 40 sagenes wide and 80 long, and in some places even more, sowing which with grain they reckon on two quarters per dessiatine, and otherwise one and a half quarters. At the sowing of spring grain also a certain quantity is suggested, in some places more and in others less.[3] Unjust and self-interested bailiffs, elected officials and elders, can in this case carry out no small misappropriation every year, if there is not the proper supervision of them here; because, subtracting several sagenes from the defined dessiatine, they can do the peasants a favour easily and in an undetected manner, and at sowing time every year hide and steal some seed grain. Because of this, the good steward or bailiff should measure the landlord's dessiatines without imposing upon anybody, and as an experiment sowing several dessiatines, make observations, so that there is no reduction in the landlord's fields, and no theft of seed grain; but it is not possible to prescribe exactly how many quarters to sow per dessiatine. A new steward or bailiff, after finding out how they sowed before his arrival, should sow a number of dessiatines with a certain reduction, and according to the harvest bring the whole sowing to the exactness demanded by the nature of the land and the air; because there occur not only very thick but also very thin sowings that are unsuccessful if done without any supervision. It is necessary also to see that for driving cattle in and out near the villages, there should be a special enclosure or fence, so that cattle being driven out from the houses or back from the fields will not break into areas that are sown, and there will not be damage from them. This should be particularly guarded against when the grain is ripening, with appointment for the purpose of special watchmen from the old people, to whom young children can be added as help. With us usually and everywhere such enclosures are composed of barriers made of rails and bindings, and in some places of wattle fences, but it will be much better and more lasting if they start in place of bound and wattle fences to make ditches, one and a half to two arshines deep, and five or six quarters wide. These ditches once made demand little attention every year. And cattle will not be allowed not only to break into the fields, but also to stray from their homes and disappear. They will serve also towards the preservation of the woods; because for the repair of enclosure bindings, quite a number of rails, consequently not a little timber, are always necessary.

5

There is an old practice with us, to apportion the able-bodied peasants by households, counting as a household the man and his wife (and excluding the crippled and the aged from the households), dividing among them the land where it is not super-abundant, and where, moreover, it is not possible to plough it as much as necessary. In these great inequalities are created by self-interested stewards and bailiffs, and particularly from elders and elected officials; because an apportionment once carried out remains with us for a long time irrespective of the fact that by the various circumstances of the estate, they sometimes have to be increased or decreased, observing between all the best possible equality. For this a new steward or bailiff commencing the management of villages, not adding to the number of households that existed before his arrival and already communicated to him, must make a household list of all peasants, including the male sex and the female, not excluding minors with a note of their age, and of those who are in a household or retired from household labour, or not yet apportioned to a household. And whoever is more than sixteen years old should be put into household labour,[4] even though they are unmarried, because it is sufficiently obvious that many parents, not wanting their children to be in household labour, and so that they may lounge about among the minors and non-apportioned, do not concern themselves about the marriage of their sons and even more of their daughters, and divert them from it in every way possible. But if it is necessary to marry any of the unfortunates, they borrow the lord's malt for the brewing of beer for this feast, and if there is no horse for ploughing and horse work, then they must give him one of the lord's horses, possibly a cow and a sheep too, so that he will be in a position to carry out as much of the lord's work and his own as the others, and with his wife have a reasonable subsistence. So that these young people will carry out their obligations better, and not exhaust the lord's horses that have been given them, instead of sending them to the landlord's work at ploughing time, send them more to those places where itinerant workers are in demand. This inspection and apportionment of households should be made every year by the stewards and bailiffs, and everything possible should be done every two or three years. Peasants will be added or subtracted according to the number of households available in the new register, and the stewards and bailiffs must tell their lords about this. And it would be good, if they would at the same time point out how many are newly married, born or dead, so that each landlord will know the condition of his villages. In a word: a steward or bailiff zealous about the interest of his lord must always try to increase the number of peasants in the households, and not exclude from their number any but the crippled, the very old and the unsuited for the lord's work in all respects: even these should not be left without a job, but used to their utmost capability in various kinds of rural superintendence, as mentioned above, giving them as help young children, who are not apportioned to households, and whoever is excluded from the households for whatever reason. And the lord should be informed about whether everybody is apportioned to his place or not.

6

In the use of household peasants for the lord's work, we act according to the wish of the landlords. There are some so severe, that they do not allow their peasants to work one day for themselves; and giving all their families monthly provisions, they use them without exception for the lord's work every day. Others work four days a week for the landlord, and three days including Sunday are left to them. Those who are maintained in a moderate manner work three days for the landlord, and as many days for themselves, and Sunday remains for rest. But tilling is improved more by assignments. Per household, some till more than two dessiatines, others two, one and a half, or one. Apportioning the lord's and the peasants' days by fields, some enforce the tilling prescribed for the lord in each field, not allowing one day off until all is done, and then they allow the peasants to do their own. A humane lord who really loves his native land will never order his stewards and bailiffs to impose on each household more than one dessiatine, and certainly not more than one and a half dessiatines, for ploughing, sowing and keeping tidy in each field. From this he will get enough profit when the land is promptly and well ploughed and sown. And they will reap his grain at the proper time and put it on the threshing floor; because the peasant must plough and sow at least two or three times the above for himself and for sale to the public (in payment of state taxes, etc.) And although a diligent household peasant will sow more for his lord, what is the use of it, when he will not plough the land well, and will prematurely harvest and take to the threshing floor the grain that he has sown?

7

Although assigned tasks such as all cultivation generally, weeding and harvesting of grain, haymaking, etc., are considered very profitable for peasants and landlords alike; all the same the stewards and bailiffs both themselves and through the peasant elders should diligently see that all the tasks are done with the proper care and not negligently, and particularly should watch with a vigilant eye[5] the tilling, sowing and harvesting of grain, that the earth is ploughed properly and more deeply and well harrowed,[6] and that the peasants who are used for the sowing of grain are skilled in this, and throw the seeds on the earth evenly, not often and not infrequently, particularly so that there should not be clumps or bare patches. For this purpose, as the first and most necessary matter, appoint from the best old men those who are sufficiently experienced in cultivation, assuring them that if there will be a bad germination and harvest from the seed sown, and a good grain appears on their own dessiatines, then that will be taken for the lord, and the bad grain given to them as a punishment. At the same time, the bailiffs and the stewards, likewise the elected officials and the elders must diligently observe that all the tasks for the lord are carried out, not wasting any suitable time.

8

As far as the assignment of peasants is concerned as elected officials, elders, clerks for income and expenditure, and other district farm and village duties; on big estates, this can be left to the choice and judgement of the bailiffs and the elected officials, unless the landlord himself wants to use any of his peasants for this or that job because of his knowledge and confidence, and this may always be left to his discretion. When these people are assigned to their duties by the choice of the commune and the judgement of the stewards and bailiffs, then they must be responsible for them in case of their neglect. In less large and small villages, elected officials and elders are determined by the choice of the people of the commune, and the whole commune should be responsible for them. So that people suitable for these tasks can always be found, select one or two of the children mentioned above, who (according to the second of these points) have learned to read and write, and are cleverer than the others, so that they may be instructed for those tasks which they will carry out later, and they will be used profitably at their maturity, and the stewards and bailiffs can keep them in turn for a week for this purpose, or as is considered suitable.

9

Many of the great families have such large villages, that they are equal to towns of a considerable size. In such large places, the steward or bailiff must without fail institute a system similar to the police.[7] Assigning to small groups of households tithingmen, and for a hundred or possibly two hundred households one hundreder, from the best and most diligent people, give them useful instructions on how to keep good order among the inhabitants and peace in each hundred; and so that suspicious people do not creep into the mass of the inhabitants, so that there are no wilful distant absences, flights, etc., command them to ascertain daily or every week that everything in their area is quiet, and that nothing extraordinary has occurred; and, more than this, have a guard from each hundred at the lord's house for security and for summoning the hundreders; this arrangement seems absolutely necessary in large settlements, and for the eradication of all theft, and for precaution in case of fire, particularly in case of horse and cattle plague, and in other extraordinary circumstances, these tithingmen and hundreders can be replaced by others every year, or every third of a year.

10

The increase of farmers is considered a most important point not only for the landlords but for the whole state, and nothing is more conducive to this, than the timely marriage of young people, and moderate labour and reasonable upkeep for them. With our peasantry for a long time past and in many places there has been the custom of marrying young boys to grown girls, which marriages produce not profit but harm and discord, and there is not here the least means of increasing the people, nor of good household management, and therefore it should not be allowed. Wise stewards and bailiffs must attempt to see to it (as was mentioned also above in point 5) that young people of more than eighteen years of age from the peasantry, at most more than twenty, should not lounge about single. When such people are noticed, encourage their fathers and them themselves towards marriage, looking in the villages for girls of their age, and even two or three years younger than them; but because it not infrequently happens that in one village there are more young people of the male sex, and in another more girls, therefore the landlords must give permission to their stewards and bailiffs for the delivery of grown girls to other villages, assigning a quantity of money for their transfer, where it is arranged on both sides, and marry young men to girls without transfer money but do not forbid such a loan. As far as transfer money is concerned, it seems enough for the landlord to allow from ten to fifteen roubles to be paid for the delivered girl, only it should be given with the consent of the stewards and bailiffs, and in their absence with that of the elders and elected officials with written testimony and the agreement of the fathers and mothers on both sides, and without any infringement of freedom. But if such a young man refuses a marriage, or his father and mother are not inclined towards it through any weakness, in that case he must be forced to it in the proper manner.

11

As regards the peasantry, both for themselves and society as a whole, no trade or craft can be as useful or as profitable as agriculture; because its return on the capital used is not only twofold, but three and five; sometimes a tenfold profit accrues, but there is the peculiarity that work carried on in agriculture is disproportionately more burdensome and laborious in comparison with other trades and crafts, and this is often with us the reason that many of the peasants, and particularly those prone to idleness and laziness, absenting themselves from agriculture, take up various kinds of commerce and trade, from which there is very little advantage for them, and no profit for society. Especially those prone to idleness and laziness, to the great harm of themselves and society, go away to distant districts for a long time, lounge about as parasites and fall into various debaucheries.[8] Therefore, in those estates on which there is enough land for agriculture and on whose appurtenances there is enough upkeep for cattle, and where there is no impoverishment of the rural Economy as a whole, stewards and bailiffs must act very carefully in the matter of permission to peasants to trade in goods which do not belong to them and to have such trades and crafts as are not suitable for them, and above all force them towards agriculture, that is towards the increase of their own arable land and that of the landlords, unless permission to the contrary is given by the judgement of the landlords themselves. However, the trades most needful and necessary in the farms and villages should not only be not forbidden but encouraged to be set up, according to the number of people and potentiality of the estate, so that each farm and village should have its own masters for its most necessary needs: for example, for each twenty or thirty households, it is not too much when there are two to three good carpenters, a blacksmith, a tailor for peasant clothing, and the like,[9] who, if there are no odd jobs to be done for the lord, must be together with others in the work of the households; but those places where there is not enough land, meadow, forest and other appurtenances for the rural Economy, should be excepted from the rule. In such cases, the landlords, stewards and bailiffs may devise the means which seem to them best and most profitable for the upkeep and enrichment of their people.

12

It is already known, that with the great size of the Russian Empire, the fertilisation of land is not necessary in certain places; on the other hand, in many districts it is absolutely necessary. As far as the first are concerned, instead of fertilising and manuring, diligent rural inhabitants who care about agriculture (adapting themselves to the population and size of the lands) plough up several dessiatines of disused land that has never been tilled before. For, however good the land is, after ten, twenty and in some cases after thirty years and more of tillage, it loses its growing power, produces shrubs and roots which hamper the seeds that are sown, and greatly hinder their growth. Taking note of this, the stewards and bailiffs must be careful in tilling unused lands about the gradual preparation of new dessiatines, which in the lower regions the peasants call stripping off the deposit. They say that such work is better and more capably done in spring, not allowing the young grass to spread its roots (from which the ploughing is more difficult). However, some peasants strip off the deposit in the autumn, and profitably prepare it for the spring sowing, and the old dessiatines, which have been tilled more than the others, are left idle. On such newly cultivated land, grain always grows better and stronger. After the old dessiatines have rested for ten or fifteen years (which is called here long fallow), they are made suitable for sowing, and in such a manner cultivation is carried on in good and fertile places, and sowing in a profitable manner without manuring. The diligent stewards and bailiffs, elders and elective officials must see that this is done in equal measure to the lands of the lord. As far as those places are concerned, where manuring and fertilisation of the lands are absolutely necessary, various methods are used by us according to the locality and nature of the land, which, if all described in detail, would demand not a little space, and everything has already been described in the works of the Free Economic Society.[10] The rural stewards must become familiar with these and use them, without wasting suitable times; because in agriculture neglect and wastage of times suitable for it always produce poor consequences, that is crop failure, all kinds of loss and harm.

13

Similarly in the harvesting of grain, particularly in the placing of it on the threshing floor in sheaves and stooks, there are many various habits according to the different provinces.[11] It must not be prescribed, which of these is the best and most apt for every case; this depends more on the condition of the area and on those making up the institution and on the skill of the supervisors. In general it seems that the Ukrainian and Tartar practice of placing grain stooks on frames three quarters from the ground is very useful, and brings them to completion more quickly; because they do not decay or rot underneath from the ground, and not only damp harms them, so not only will grain be stacked dry (because damp and wet grain placed in stooks and loads rots and is wasted) but also mice cannot so easily slip into these stooks. In many places it often happens with us that much unthreshed grain is ruined because of all kinds of damp getting into it and mice making nests in it because the sheaves and stooks are placed on the ground unevenly and askew. Stewards and bailiffs should be warned to try to choose ways and means which would serve to the better preservation of the charge entrusted to them by their lord, and for this they must often themselves supervise these tasks, not leaving it to the elected officials and the elders. And because they must make an estimate about the grain harvest, or an approximate calculation beforehand, they must order their elected officials and elders to see that each peasant places an equal number of sheaves on his cart for carriage to the threshing floor, and to list in the estate records how many loads there have been in each cart. And so that the quantity of grain may be more exactly known, then during the harvesting of every variety, take some of the good, the average and the bad for a sample threshing, make a note of the weight of each grain and from that an estimate, informing the lord at the beginning of a new year, so that he will know how much grain there is on hand at his estate.

14

There is an old custom in all our farms and villages to make storing barns by digging a hole in the ground and making a stove in it, from which the barn warms up and the grain placed in it gets dry. And so hardly a year passes by without barns burning up in this manner, and sometimes it happens that the people threshing get burned up, the harm from which is known to everybody and does not need explanation. Apart from this evil, closed threshing floors are rarely to be found, and so rain, snow and all kinds of bad weather hamper our threshing, and if such poor weather lasts for long, then the peasants often suffer a shortage of grain for their own subsistence, and for the purchase of it at markets there are often high prices. As far as the construction of better barns is concerned, an instruction has already been drawn up for the public by the Economic Society;[12] but it will be even better, when diligent stewards and bailiffs will try at the first opportunity to build threshing barns if only for the landlord's grain after the model of how they are made here in Livonia and Ingermanland, using for such construction rough stone and brick, where it is not difficult to obtain it, and, where it is not to be found, then wood. From this little by little the peasants, and particularly the older ones, will acquire the habit, and will have threshing floors covered in every possible way, by bast, shingles or where necessary by thatch, so that threshing can be carried on at all times, and be freed from those complications which are referred to above.

15

Each steward or bailiff must be thoroughly informed not only about what there is on his lord's estate, but also about what there is not, and for this purpose he should know about not only the boundaries and limits but also about their contents, that is, where there are any appurtenances, arable land, hay fields and other assets, and he should ensure that the best possible income and return is made for the lord. For example, surplus lands and meadows, where there are some, should be rented to other people; in the lakes and ponds, if there are or could be some, fishing should be commenced, some of the subordinate lord's household people and peasants being taught for this purpose and for the manufacture of fishing tackle; on the rivers, mills may be constructed, or such places leased for construction and upkeep for a certain number of years with appropriate payment. On the large estates, where there are sufficient woods, the landlords may be recommended to set up distilleries and sawmills, or river boats and craft and the like can be made, attempts being made to increase the income of the lord in all possible ways. When there is no field work for women and girls and young boys, and there are berries, nuts, mushrooms, hops and other such items in the woods, then, not wasting useful time, order them to be collected, and turn this also to the lord's advantage. Try to introduce and increase fruitful gardens, bees and the like: in a word, not to let slip that which brings great or small profit to the landlord from the potential of the estate entrusted to him, he can do the smaller business by himself, and let his landlord know about the large as indicated above and wait for orders, unless he has been given full authority for decisions on everything. Beyond this, they must concern themselves with the landlord's houses and gardens, with each building of the estate, their good condition, cleanliness and (depending on the condition of the estate and the lord) their arrangement and keep ready for any situation the necessary supplies.[13]

16

The upkeep of horses and all kinds of cattle in rural household management is almost as necessary a part of the Economy as agriculture itself, particularly in those places where there are enough places for haymaking and pasturing, and where manure is used for the fertilisation of lands. Therefore, the diligent steward or bailiff must try to the advantage of both the estate and the pasture lands to keep a horse stud, and all kinds of cattle, building in advance the appropriate shelters, according to the well-known proverb: build a cattle shed first, and then start to keep cattle. Make sure that for horses in wintertime there are warm and well-covered stables, stalls and barns, and for horned cattle cow houses and sheds, so that they will always be kept clean and there will be bedding and sufficient feed for horses, mares and foals, and for horned cattle large and small. As far as a horse stud is concerned, no little space is necessary for a description of all its accessories, and there is already such a special description, which the steward or bailiff must find and adhere to. Care for horned cattle and birds [has been] according to established custom, although the worst and most stupid people are used here, sometimes in place of a fine. Abandoning this, choose the best and most reliable people from the male and female sex, accustom them with kindness to good tending, teach them with clear and intelligible explanations when and how to look after cattle, collect wool, accumulate milk, take off the cream and make butter from it (of which good farm workers give a pood per year) and so on. Turn all this to the advantage of the landlord, with its sale or dispatch to him, and see that nothing is wasted from it.

17

If cattle or horse plague breaks out, act in such cases with the power of the decrees published about it (in which all the needs to be taken care of are prescribed) without omission, irrespective of the complaints and dissatisfaction of the peasantry; because it often happens that from their carelessness and inadequate supervision in many places, all the horses and horned cattle die. Therefore the stewards and bailiffs must try to see that those estates which according to the poll-tax assessment have no less than two or three hundred souls permanently possess a farrier, the trade being taught to some lord's household people or capable peasants in those places where reputable and skilful farriers are to be found. Medicines and drugs useful for this must be stocked, and kept in readiness for the necessary eventualities. For the better preservation of horses, and particularly of mares and foals, on dark nights, when bears and wolves often do them harm, they must be driven nearer to the houses and kept in herds, and such herds may be formed in the steppe when strong, suitable places and a vigilant guard are chosen.

18

It is well known, that in our villages there are many poor thatched roofs,[14] and instead of candles they almost everywhere burn torches, and often cause great fires from carelessness, with the flames from which many rural inhabitants are ruined and others perish. Stewards and bailiffs must often reaffirm that it is always and everywhere necessary to act carefully with fire, and particularly in summertime, when there are great heatwaves and droughts, to warm up huts and baths should be prohibited. For the cooking of food far from habitation and near water order special stoves to be made; and if after the order has been given somebody dares to heat his hut or bath, punish him at a meeting as a warning to the others. I myself was a witness last year in 1769 to a fire being made by reason of the drought from the small sparks of a single hot ash thrown carelessly from a stove, and a great number of farms and villages have been burnt up in this manner. Thus the inhabitants were completely ruined, and went about the commune like beggars and were fed on the commune's charity.

19

It is no less necessary to take precautions against forest fires, particularly in time of drought, and for that give strict orders that not only in the forests themselves but even in proximity to them working people may not make fires, and if anywhere in the forest unexpectedly catches fire and there is smoke, then quickly suppress and extinguish it with all available strength. Moreover, for their conservation act carefully in the felling of them, do not henceforth cut down for firewood timber suitable for construction, and do not leave in the forest the top and twigs of trees felled for construction, but order them and each windfall to be carried away and used for firewood or whatever else appropriate. And for this purpose appoint one or two woodmen or patrolmen from the peasants. On the big estates where there are enough woods, try to teach them to saw with handsaws instead of making rough planks with axes, and this will lead to the economical use and conservation of timber. Beyond this, in those places where there is a shortage of woods, diligent stewards and bailiffs can easily start them by planting rose and white willow stakes, driving them into the ground, which, as is generally known, take easily and quickly without roots. But if the soil anywhere is dry, of clay or sand, here at first it is necessary to water them, using for this purpose the young people of the male and female sex, if such a plantation is not far from water. This work can be carried out more reliably in autumn, however it is not impossible in the spring as soon as the snow has thawed. Stakes for spring must be prepared before the descent of winter.[15] Other kinds of woods (where there are no skilful people to produce them from seeds) may be obtained for transplanting from the nearest places, selecting for this the smallest trees, of which no small number can be placed on one cart. Those planted in autumn also take root well.

20

It has been pointed out above (in point 6) that the peasants of each household must work fixed days for their lord. When field and other regular work does not occur, in those places where there are enough woods, the steward may send them to cut trees and firewood and to burn charcoal, and if it is not necessary for the lord's consumption, send it for sale to the nearest markets or as considered more suitable, and putting the money collected in this manner in the receipts, keep it for necessary rural expenses, as will be ordered by the landlord. Moreover, if there is a way of making an income for the lord from the catching of animals or fish, then do not let this slip by. In a word, a diligent and faithful steward, without direction about everything, strives to achieve advantage and profit for his lord according to the circumstances of the estate entrusted to him, because it is impossible to recommend and include all details in this instruction.

21

In many places there is the custom that each female peasant of each household must spin and weave twelve arshines of linen and cloth, and in some estates they impose more on them, which is all considered to be quitrent; it is made of the lord's wool, flax or hemp, and if there is no domestic supply on his estate, then it is bought and distributed; but if they do not weave linen, then the cloth quitrent is doubled, and instead of 12 arshines, they ask for 24 or 20 arshines of full-size cloth from one woman. The steward and bailiff or rather their wives (because we consider this woman's work) should try to see that this point is properly carried out as written above, or as specially ordered by the landlord. If there is not any wool, flax and hemp, then buy it at the markets and distribute it among the peasants in the autumn. Taking in linen and cloth, see that it is woven properly and not coarsely. Therefore for inspection and delivery assign one of the best peasant women who is capable and reliable. As the cloth is being taken in, write it into the accounts, and send it off to the lord, or sell it for the increase of the village income, as ordered by the lord.

22

Good stewards and bailiffs see that peasant children from ten years and more use their time for the advantage of the lord and the peasants, and do not accustom themselves to idleness through lazily lounging about. Above (point 2) it is pointed out that several of them should be taught to read books, and some of them to write as well. Apart from this, they may be used according to their age for various uses as indicated above and announced in the works of the Free Economic Society.[16] To put it in a word: it is necessary that these young and immature people should work according to their capacities, at least have the habit of it, and never be in idleness from which great harm would result.

23

Although peasants on quitrent are not without use both for themselves and their landlords, there is no great profit in them for society, and a great loss is incurred particularly for agriculture with their absence from their homes for trades in distant towns and settlements. For this reason, in those places where there is enough land, it is more suitable to keep them farming, as pointed out in point 11 above; but in those places, where there is an insufficiency of land and appurtenances, the quitrent livelihood of the peasants is necessary: moreover, if it is noticed that there is a particular inclination and capacity for useful trades and crafts, it is not useful to hold them back, because one prosperous, manufacturing peasant may lend to many poor ones and give them subsistence. But the number of such quitrent people should not be great, and those engaged in agriculture should always be more, and so that nobody should want to go on quitrent in those places where there is no shortage of land, for this it is not unreasonable to levy a heavy quitrent, at least no less than five roubles a year on each household, or as fixed by the landlord himself, and passports should not be given for more than two years or for all families, and they should not be allowed from the estate least they forget and leave their natural habitat.

24

Among the peasants there are sometimes some who are so negligent that they concern themselves little and badly with their own household management; and particularly they do not keep their horses and cattle in the proper care and condition, and thus fall into extreme poverty, into dissipation, into flight and thievery. Therefore, the stewards and bailiffs should find out about each peasant, how he observes the management of his household. How does he keep his horses and cattle, and how does he apply himself to agriculture? Those who are negligent should be summoned and reprimanded, cowered and impressed upon that they should go about their household management more efficiently and diligently; from time to time, visit them and their houses, encouraging their household management, their setting up of vegetable gardens, fruit orchards and the like. If anybody keeps his outbuildings badly, if there is a lot of manure in his stable and cattle sheds, a lot of filth in his yard, overworked and emaciated horses and cattle, punish him at a meeting of all the peasants, and bring them into a better condition and supervise their cultivation. And specifically: that their dessiatines are well ploughed and fertilised, and that the sowing is done properly. If there are such who will not be diligent in their agriculture after such exhortations and measures, and remain prone to idleness, squabbles and other lack of self-discipline, order some of such young and healthy people to be given as recruits in case of levies; and those who are older, send for settlement in distant places according to the power of the laws for the restraint and intimidation of the others, obtaining receipts for their inclusion in the recruits, so that there will be no temptation to others from such spongers and squabblers. However beforehand it is necessary to write about them to the landlords, and ask orders for it from them, or in case of their distant absence, proceed with the agreement of the elected officials, elders and best peasants, and not by oneself. And those peasants who apply themselves more and better than others to agriculture and to household management should be treated with obvious kindness and preference before the lazy and negligent. Particularly when recruit levies take place, do not give them and their children as recruits, unless there is the most extreme necessity.

25

Stewards and bailiffs should also try to see that in the estates entrusted to them the weights and measures should be correct in comparison with those of the state. Never allow wilful divergences from the state weights and measures, because when they are not comparable to the state's there are many deceits and thefts, and it is not possible to compile accurate accounts of income and expense.

26

It remains to refer to two important conditions which good stewards and bailiffs must in my opinion diligently observe. One of them concerns the supervision of the health of the farm and village inhabitants under their authority. And secondly, there is no less of a necessity, when a grain harvest failure occurs, for reserve grain to be loaned to poor peasants. As far as the first is concerned, it must be reaffirmed to all peasant women, and they must be supervised in this, that in their cottages they observe the greatest possible cleanliness, being careful about unclean and poisonous air, and taking particular care about serious and catching illnesses. Each settlement should have good midwives as skilful as possible so that in cases of difficult births they should know how to facilitate them. Women in an advanced stage of pregnancy should not be detailed to heavy work, and should try to have with them old men and women, who by long experience of illnesses which occur can help with various tested herbs and rural domestic methods. In necessary cases under their authority should be those who know how to let blood, how to use the clyster and the like, and to keep the necessary instruments for this.[17] As far as the second point is concerned, about the institution in all villages of reserve grain for loan to very poor peasants in cases of such occurrences as poor harvest, the stewards and bailiffs must have an annual concern. In my opinion, in an imperceptible manner and one completely unburdensome for the peasants, at the end of each sowing, harvesting and storing of grain prescribed by the landlord, all the peasants must be forced every year to work together one day, that is to plough and sow, harvest and store away, by means of which I hope in not many years the necessary grain reserve will be made in each village, and the capital can be collected not only for loan to the poor and needy, but also for church and other rural general expenses, without any burden to the landlords or the peasants. As far as this point is concerned, a direction about this can be read in the second part of the works of the Economic Society, printed on the first and following pages, to which I refer you.

27

Nevertheless, each steward or bailiff must act according to the decrees published and being published to the people, collect them and keep them with great care, so that on the estate entrusted to him nothing occurs in contravention to them, and the state taxes are paid without arrears. Make an assessment for this payment, so that it should not be more burdensome to the poor than to the rich; and particularly in respect of lost souls, who should be levied on the prosperous and the tradesmen, without weighing them down with the poor and those with large families. This cannot be exactly and comprehensively recommended for all stewards and bailiffs, and it must be left to their own judgement, to strongly observe that there is no theft and flights, and that they do not have in their settlements refuges for runaways, suspicious and thieving people, who, whenever they apppear, should be caught and sent to the places assigned for their committal according to the laws with the appropriate report, when and by whom they were caught and where they were sent. Trial and punishment in peasant affairs and quarrels must be carried out impartially, but according to actual justice, and apart from the income allowed to the lord from the peasants, no requisitions or bribes should be extorted.

There still remains something of that which should be prescribed for the duties of the steward and bailiff, and that written above, I think, demands much explanation and proof. But having already filled more than five sheets with this work, I shall try to supplement it in the future, if this be considered a good thing. Meanwhile, I conclude with our well-known proverb: While you live, learn and work.

Rychkov's footnotes (not numbered in the original)
1. I have decided not to discuss here the qualities of stewards or bailiffs, because

that would not be an instruction for them, but for the landlords themselves. It is enough if they choose people who are conscientious, sober and informed as much as possible about the rural Economy, and know how to read and write, and know well how to do accounts, and are diligent in reading the Economic books, which their landlords should themselves give them, as well as such upkeep that they will not look for prohibited income to the oppression of their subordinates. They should carry out everything according to state laws which they must observe unfailingly and everything from these points which is to the advantage and interest of the lord, not weakening anybody but giving in everything a true and just account. I do not put anything in these points if it is superfluous, but it may be, like my other observations placed under the lines here, excluded. The instruction composed by Baron Wolff printed in Part XII of the Economic Works, I have read before sending off the composition, and there is in my opinion much in it that is necessary and useful.

2. I have purposely described here a steward or bailiff newly entered upon his charge, in order to show how he must begin and continue the supervision entrusted to him. However what is described here to stewards and bailiffs applies also in their absence to elected village officials and elders.

3. In answers to questions of the Free Economic Society already published is information about where how much grain and of what type is sown in each dessiatine.

4. Household peasant labour means with us that when a peasant for a fixed time equally with others ploughs, sows, harvests and threshes, mows hay, working three days for the landlord so that nothing is lacking, or in place of all this pays quitrent in money. Old men are not included in the household, but are used for light work, and more for keeping watch as church sextons, in mills, at the threshing of grain, at granaries, on guard in the fields or at the outskirts of the village and so on, and to help them are sometimes added some young people who are not yet enrolled in the household.

5. Peasants who are lazy and prone to deceit do many mean tricks during these appointed tasks, specifically: when they plough they try to do a short furrow and fill it in with a layer of earth or loose earth; when they sow, they throw the seed incorrectly and make bare patches in some places, so the grain does not grow and there are empty spaces; during the time of reaping and harvest, they trample the grain right down into the ground, so that their deceit cannot be discerned. Therefore in this work a watch must be kept on them every hour, and when they reap barley, it is good to send young boys to collect ears which have fallen on the ground, because the ears of this grain particularly when overripe are easily broken off and piled up in great quantities on the ground.

6. I consider it a very good procedure in agriculture if instead of our normal harrows with wooden teeth we attach to them iron teeth, with which the earth is much better and more gently fertilised.

7. By this word are meant turnpikes, watches with batons in useful places at appropriate times and with firefighting instruments arranged in the proper manner. It would be useful to collect all the decrees concerning the rural Economy and the police, so that nobody should err against them.

8. You can read about this in Part VI of the Economic Works, pp.56ff.

9. Added to the above mentioned trades should be a tanner for the processing of sheepskins, a potter, a brickmaker, a turner of large and small wooden bowls, dishes, plates and spoons, the making of weaving reeds, traps to catch animals and fish and so on, which must be done all winter between the busy

seasons. However it is the first and most necessary business for each peasant to know how to make and properly assemble a plough, a harrow and everything necessary for husbandry and horse harness.

NB. In some places it happens that some peasants not only in winter but in summer time stay away from their residence and go off in groups leading bears which they teach to dance, and they play about with them and fall into various bad ways, leaving agriculture completely. This harmful business should be completely prohibited, and no peasant should be allowed to take it up.

10. In respect of this it would be useful if conscientious landlords supplied their estates with editions of these works already published and to be published in the future about the rural Economy emphasising to their stewards and bailiffs that at appropriate times they should act according to them. It would be very advisable that stewards and bailiffs should learn to do all sorts of Economic experiments on their estates and observe atmospheric changes, keeping a daily record of these and of all rural production.

11. Threshing floors with us are usually near the settlements and villages. But in Siberia the sheaves and stooks are put up in the fields in the middle of the cultivated plot, so that the carrying of sheaves and the construction of stooks can be more easily carried out. This practice is very good, and serves to no small lightening of the busy times of the peasants. I myself follow this in respect of my own growing, but it is suitable only on those estates where there is one landlord and not many and where there is no danger of theft.

12. See Part IV of the works of that Society, p.65ff.

13. It is very necessary for us to have in the villages timber reserves in consideration of the fires which occur, so that from them the necessary construction can take place. I myself after the fire I was present at, from which my own house burnt down to the ground, suffered great hardship since I had no reserve timber. My domestics and my young children suffered great difficulty from it, and the new house had to be built from damp new wood.

14. Thatched roofs made in the German manner I consider not harmful, but on the contrary most useful in timberless places, and our peasants should be taught this.

15. It would be good and useful if our peasants should learn how to plant stakes for this quickly growing wood around their homes and gardens, which growing in size may serve as protection and a ready defence, and also be used in the making of wattle fences instead of the present ones, on which too much of all kinds of timber is used.

16. On these matters, in which at the beginning of spring, in summer and up to autumn young peasant children of both sexes may be used, see the works of the aforementioned Society, Part IV p.57, Part V p.46, Part VI p.69, Part IX p.75ff. Many other kinds of light work for them might easily be found. It mostly depends on the consideration of the stewards and bailiffs and their wives.

17. The domestic medical guide of Mr. Peken dedicated to the Members of the Economic Society and already twice published is everywhere a necessary book, in respect of this point for its clarity and the many simple methods to be found in almost all villages. Gentlemen landlords should act sensibly as far as this point is concerned, if by this and other publications useful for rural life they would furnish their stewards and bailiffs, with the order that they should use and try to teach the methods prescribed in them.

From *Trudy vol'nogo ekonomicheskogo obshchestva k pooshchreniiu v Rossii zemledeliia i domostroitel'stva*, XVI, 1770.

8. The Pugachev Revolt, 1773-5

   a) **Popular Satire**
   b) **The Edicts of Pugachev**
   c) **Governmental Manifestos on Pugachev**
   d) **Pugachev's Testimony at the Interrogation in Iaik Town, 16 September 1774**
   e) **A Contemporary Noble writes about Pugachev**

INTRODUCTION

Upper-class attitudes to the peasantry in the late eighteenth century varied. On the one hand, there was the enlightened view represented above in the Prize Essay of A. Ia. Polenov. Conceding that "Everybody knows to what great vices the common people is usually subject: ignorance, superstition, intemperance, idleness, thoughtlessness make us not only contemptuous of it, but sometimes hate it," he did not agree that the "best way . . . of holding back its violent folly, is severity, force and executions," pointing out that "this might lead to the aggravation rather than the cure of the wounds." Instead, he emphasised that "to enlighten people with teaching, preserves its health by the inculcation of diligence and by physical exercises, sets them on the path of a virtuous life with the help of a healthy moral training." A certain amount of implicit agreement with such a view was expressed at the Legislative Commission, where the Bishop of Rostov and Iaroslavl supported the institution of peasant schools through which "knowledge of the Christian law will be inculcated, and the coarseness of their manners will be corrected and various lawless deeds . . . will be eradicated,"[1] and Peter Orlov, a noble deputy, described how, believing that enlightened knowledge was extremely necessary for the spiritual animal that was man, he had set up a primary school on his own estate near Moscow, as a result of which his young serfs now realised far better than before their duties to God, their sovereign, their fatherland, and their landlord.

Towards the other end of the spectrum of opinion was Prince M. M. Shcherbatov, whose already negative attitude towards the peasantry was intensified by his experience of the huge revolt that we are about to examine. At that time, in a work on Russian pretenders commissioned by Catherine, he wrote that "Though science, enlightenment and religion itself seem to have produced many alterations in our morals, yet Man's inner nature is always the same." And so revolts were recurrent crises of the body politic, "the dangerous but sometimes inevitable misadventures to which all kingdoms and powers in the world are subject," consequences of the inherent and ineradicable coarseness and gullibility of the ignorant multitude. In his "Thoughts on the disadvantages of granting freedom to the peasants in Russia or of allowing them to own lands," which were composed in 1785 four years before the onset of the French Revolution and five years before his own death, he declared:

"I leave it to the consideration of every right-thinking person. Will it be just to take away property, acquired for blood, service, toil and money — from the landowners, who comprise the most useful part of the citizens of the state, and thereby to destroy — I do not say the fundamental laws of the Russian state (for there are none), but the fundamental laws of natural justice, the same law on which all societies are founded."

Looking back at the Pugachev Revolt, he blamed Catherine herself for helping to bring it about by "destroying the bond, which existed for many centuries, between the peasants and their masters." Far from producing fundamental laws of the Russian state, the Legislative Commission of 1767 through its discussion of the peasant question had "spread a plague in the hearts of the common people," and "A spirit of insubordination and dissoluteness implanted itself in coarse and insubordinate hearts."[2]

We are not quite so ignorant as is sometimes assumed about the attitudes of the peasants themselves to questions such as those we have just been discussing. In "The Slaves' Lament", the first of the pieces of popular satire to be found below, specific reference is made to the Legislative Commission:

"They are changing the laws now for their own advantage;
They are not electing the slaves as deputies for that very reason;
What may slaves say there?"

The Lament goes on to make a possible if oblique reference to the emancipation decree of 1762, while the lines immediately preceding these just quoted might refer to the decree of 22 August 1767 restricting the right of serfs to complain against their masters. Some of the other allusions are obscure, those towards the end of the piece concerning an incident at "Dedelovo", for example (which could refer to the inundation of Dedilovo — a village in Tula province, and its permanent replacement by a lake). The general mood of the piece is unmistakable enough, however, and the wish to follow the "true tsar" already apparent.

The basic despair and resignation of "The Slaves' Lament" contrast with the wishful thinking of the second sample of popular satire, "The Dvorianin and the Muzhik", a straight-forward reversal of the kind of treatment that a peasant would normally expect to receive from a judge at a state court. A third mood, of savage revenge, is caught in the third item, "The Ox did not want to be an Ox". This verse accompanies a copper engraving made by factory-workers some time near the middle of the eighteenth century. Its mood was uppermost in the minds of the peasants during the Pugachev Revolt.

These three pieces of popular satire composed in the 1750s and 1760s, along with other examples of the genre, folk tales and broadsides, should be enough to dispel the notion that the "alternative society" during the early years of the reign of Catherine was composed of inarticulate yokels, even if the evidence is not on the other hand sufficient to compel acceptance of the notion advanced by some Soviet historians of a contemporary "serf intelligentsia."

Interestingly enough, Emel'ian Ivanovich Pugachev failed to meet one of the basic requirements for inclusion in such a group, since he was illiterate. Yet it would be wrong to dismiss him either for his inability to read and write or for his apparently absurd pretension to be Peter III. The leader of the largest civil disturbance suffered by Russian absolutism between the accession of the Romanov dynasty in 1613 and the Revolutions of the twentieth century would have to be something more than the "vile miscreant" of governmental decrees. Pugachev was born a Don Cossack in or about 1742, and first experienced military service during the Seven Years War in Prussia, where he was chosen to be orderly to a Cossack Colonel because of "outstanding adroitness." His ability and experience by the time of the Russo-Turkish War of 1768-1774 were sufficient for him to be appointed to the Cossack equivalent of company commander, and he performed bravely enough in action against the infidel. But having contracted a serious illness and managing to obtain a protracted leave for convalescence, he had no desire to return to the front, and took to flight instead. Delusions of royal grandeur may well have visited him already; he now took them to a new level.

The Cossacks of the Iaik (later Ural) River were highly annoyed at being incorporated more and more into the governmental adminstration, and had already taken their dissatisfaction to the point of violence when Pugachev came along to give their movement a figurehead and a drive which it had previously lacked. Redress for the grievances of the Cossacks and for those of the indigenous peoples allied to them is promised in the first edict of Pugachev in his new guise, a restored Peter III. Such impersonation does not appear so absurd when viewed in the tradition of a long line of pretenders making use of the "naive monarchism" of the peasantry and of other potential followers. And, deservedly or not, Peter III had posthumously gained a reputation for justice and philanthropy which Pugachev was to make full use of.

The development of the revolt may be followed through the decrees of the "great sovereign emperor ' and of the government. To begin with, the insurgents concentrated on the siege of Orenburg and other towns, while trying to bring adjacent regions into the orbit of hostilities. Pugachev appealed to a number of different people to join him: nomadic and settled tribesmen, dissident tsarist soldiers, and factory workers. The government's manifesto of 23 December 1773 recalled the Time of Troubles (Grishka Otrep'ev having been the first false Dmitrii), announced the expedition of General Bibikov to prevent its repetition, and reaffirmed faith in "intermediate authorities". In the early spring of 1774, Pugachev switched his main theatre of operations to the Ural region to consolidate new sources of support. A third and final phase of the revolt began after the rebel forces suffered a crushing defeat near Kazan, soon after they had taken that town except for its Kremlin. During the summer of 1774, thousands of peasants along the Volga and nearer the heart of the Empire rose up in the name of the pretender, even though he himself was not among them but making his way further and further downstream. The decree of 31 July depicted a kind of Cossack commonwealth with the restoration of Old Belief and the eradication of the nobility, and its appeal aroused a response which put into the hearts of Catherine and the ruling class a great terror. This was reflected in the governmental decree of 19 December 1774 and in the memoirs of a contemporary noble, A.T. Bolotov, who also wrote something about the levy of irregular forces against Pugachev and about the rebel leader's death.

Some of Pugachev's irresolution and waywardness are evident in the deposition made by him after he was handed over to tsarist troops by some of his former supporters (as is a faulty memory – a decree *was* sent to Saratov, for example). Yet at other times he had shown determination and insight. His followers were more than a completely disorganised rabble although never a match for detachments of the regular army, and the basic aims of the movement were proclaimed clearly enough. For Soviet historians, the scale of operations and the radical ideology of the Pugachev Revolt are more than sufficient for it to deserve to be called "peasant war", while at least some Western historians have felt that it would more accurately be typified as a "frontier jacquerie".

Footnotes

1. P. Dukes, *Catherine the Great*, p.208.
2. A. Lentin, ed. and trans., *On the Corruption of Morals in Russia*, Cambridge, 1969, p.52.

a)   **Popular Satire**

The Slave's Lament

O woe to us slaves living for the masters!
We do not know how to serve their ferocity!
Service is like a sharp scythe;
And kindness is like the morning dew.
O woe to us slaves from our masters, and poverty!
And when you make them angry, then they take away your patrimony.
What in the world worse than this could happen to a man?
And what we make for ourselves — even over that we have no power.
So in the whole world — there's no such vile existence!
Perhaps we had better ask Alexander Nevskii for help?
Brothers, how annoying it is to us
And how shameful and insulting
That another who is not worthy to be equal with us
Has so many of us in his power.
For as long as we miserable people may live
We miserable people will always grieve.
It seems both heaven and earth are annoyed with us!
Surely we could find ourselves grain without our masters!
For what have the woods and fields been created,
When the share of the poor has been taken away?
Why and for what were we born on to this earth?
Our fathers are guilty for having rewarded us thus.
Now the lords against the law
Do not ever believe their servants about anything!
Without us having any choice they call us poor people thieves.
"We eat bread for nothing", — they complain all the time.
And if we steal from the lord one half kopeck,
The law commands us to be killed like a louse.
And if the master steals ten thousand,
Nobody will judge who should be hanged.
The injustice of the Russian sheriffs has increased:
Whoever brings a present is right beyond argument.
They have stopped putting their trust in the Creator for authority,
And have become accustomed to own us like cattle.
All nations rebuke us and wonder at our stupidity,
That such stupid people are born in Russia.
And indeed, stupidity was rooted in us long ago,
As each honour here has been given to vagrants.
The master can kill the servant like a gelding;
The denunciation by a slave cannot be believed.

Unjust judges have composed a decree
That we should be tyrannically whipped with a knout for that.
They are changing the laws now for their own advantage;
They are not electing the slaves as deputies for that very reason,
What may slaves say there?
They have given themselves freedom to exhaust us to death.
It seems that all we unhappy people were born on earth
To be confirmed forever under the authority of such tyrants!
Why should we be tortured and grieve our whole life?
Better that we should agree to serve the tsar.
Better to live in dark woods
Than to be before the eyes of these tyrants;
They look on us cruelly with their eyes
And eat us as iron eats rye.
Not one wants to serve the tsar
But only to grind us down to the end.
And they try to collect unjust bribes,
And they are not frightened that people die cruelly.
Their power has increased, like the water in the Neva;
Wherever you look, everywhere there are lords.
Ah brothers, if we got our freedom,
We would not take the lands or the fields for ourselves.
We would go into service as soldiers, brothers,
And would be friendly among ourselves,
Would destroy all injustice
And remove the root of evil lords.
Earlier they put up with the tyrants
Because they brought enlightenment to Russia.
And now they possess us so
That slaves do not dare to speak.
When a slave dares to have words with his lord,
He has earned a beating for himself.
When they allowed the vagrants into Russia,
Then they promised us better government.
And they gave employment
To the Russian dvoriane and the smallholders,
And they divided us unfortunates up among them.
Our poor heads fell
Before evil and rapacious lords!
We are all bound by unkind hands
As if bound by such thievery.
O the evil lords will not allow us access to the tsar
And promise us no kindness.
We unfortunates have all become poor,

Better to have gone elsewhere.
Why do the slaves not get angry with them?
I think that they will soon go crazy with annoyance.
They sell all the good rye to the merchants,
And give us like pigs the bad.
The greedy lords eat meat at fast time,
And even when meat is allowed the slaves must cook meatless cabbage
    soup.
O brothers, it is our misfortune
always to have rye kasha.
The lords drink and make merry,
And do not allow the slaves even to burst out laughing.
They go to sleep on a sofa, and order everybody to move about quietly,
Not to shout or make a noise.
If anybody carelessly makes a noise,
He receives an unbearable beating.
The fear of their lord does not leave their heads;
It is as if some enemy sits behind their shoulders.
We oppose them so little, brothers,
That it seems we fear them at death!
And only when they put slaves in the grave
Do they give him a free pass.
There is no hope for slaves;
Their defenders traded them for brushwood at Dedelovo.
The rumour went around that even those dropped into a great grave
And therefore did not expect defence from anybody.
Surely there's no such empty hole in the Saratov steppe?
Only the pipe with tobacco cheers them up
And the green pea in open country.
He'd like to drink from grief a mug of wine,
But there's nowhere to get even sour beer.
The Lord our God!
Give us rest in your heavenly field!
You are our Creator;
Bring us poor people to our end.

The Dvorianin and the Muzhik

A certain dvorianin was walking ahead along a road,
And a muzhik peasant was making his way behind,
Taking firewood for sale on a horse.
He shouted to the dvorianin: Look out, sir,
I'm going along with this load, you see, move to the side.
The dvorianin pretended not to hear,
And the muzhik caught him in the back with a shaft,

117

Doing him considerable injury
And tearing his cloak.
Seeing this, the dvorianin started to quarrel with the muzhik,
Seizing him and saying: Let's go to court,
Or pay me for the cloak,
And then I won't drag you to the judge.
The muzhik cried: Enough, sir, beware,
Let me go, best not to go to court with me,
For you were wickedly haughty with me and too much so,
That's why I struck you in the back with the shaft.
The dvorianin said: No, you rogue muzhik,
I want to get my revenge on you!
Now you've started to quarrel with me,
Let's both go off to court.
And he went before the judge, and began to explain
The injury the muzhik had done him,
Saying: Your lordship, this is how
This muzhik did me injury.
I was walking along the road ahead of him,
And he was coming along behind on a horse,
And the shaft ruined my cloak,
And I demanded that he pay me for it.
I beg you to arrange
What I am asking him.
The muzhik only looks at the judge,
And does not make any speech to him.
The judge at once loudly cried
That the muzhik should make some reply.
And so he fiercely shouted: Listen, he said,
You can see the stuffed bird's guilty.
At this the judge said: I cannot make my decision
When nothing is said to me.
The dvorianin said to the judge: To tell the truth,
At the time he was going along quite boldly,
And shouted at me at the top of his voice:
Get out of the way, sir,
Can't you see that I'm going along with a load, not by myself.
Hearing this, the judge could only burst out laughing.
Why are you complaining?
You only bring shame upon yourself.
When he was polite enough to shout out at you,
Why did you not get out of the way?
And he ordered the dvorianin to be thrown out
With some good bangs on the back on the way.

And so the muzhik turned out to be right,
And the dvorianin brought upon himself the penalty.

The Ox did not want to be an Ox

The ox did not want to be an ox
And so he became a butcher.
When the butcher went to hit him on the head,
He knocked the blow aside with his horns,
And the butcher fell down.
Then the ox managed to snatch the ax from him,
Cut off his arms and hung him up by his legs,
And started to pull out the guts and lights.

From A.V. Kokorev, *Khrestomatiia po russkoi literature XVIII veka, M., 1961.*

b)   **The Edicts of Pugachev**

The First Edict of Pugachev, 17 September 1773.
Of the autocratic Emperor, our great sovereign Peter Fedorovich of all
the Russias, etc., etc., etc.

In my personal decree, it is announced to the army of the Iaik: as
you, my friends, have served former tsars to the [last] drop of your
blood, [like] your fathers and grandfathers, so you will serve me, the
great sovereign emperor Peter Fedorovich, for your fatherland.
Moreover, when you will resist for your fatherland, your Cossack glory
will not expire from now either in your lifetime or with your children.
You, Cossacks, and Kalmyks and Tartars, will be rewarded by me, the
great sovereign. And those who did wrong to me, the sovereign imperial
highness Peter Fedorovich, I, the sovereign Peter Fedorovich, forgive
you all these wrongs and I bestow on you: the river from the heights
to the mouth, and land, and meadows, and money payment, and lead,
and powder, and grain supplies.

I the great sovereign emperor, endow you.

Peter Fedorovich.

The Edict of Pugachev to the Peoples of the Urals, 1 October, 1773.
The great sovereign and tsar of tsars and worthy emperor Peter
Fedorovich, with his considered judgement send this my personal
decree to all my true subjects etc., etc., etc.

May it be known to you all, that in actuality I, I am great. And,
believing this without doubt, be assured that you on all sides and in
these parts are my subjects: Mahometans and Kalmyks, however many
you are, and all others! Being in readiness, you have to come to a
meeting with me and look on the form of my radiant face, not doing
anything unpleasing to it, and if you so choose, to do obeisance to me,
breaking your oaths. However, if there are elders among the Bashkirs
and all inhabitants of the Nogaiskaia Road, then may they come to me
in readiness, and free the people kept in prisons and with other masters
in captivity without any being left in these months and days. And the
order from me is such: if there are opponents, cut their heads off and
spill their blood, so that it might be a warning to their children. And
as your forbears, fathers and grandfathers, served my grandfather the
blessed knight and sovereign Peter Alekseevich and as you were
rewarded by him, so I now and henceforth will reward you. And I have
endowed you with land, water, salt, faith and prayer, pasture and
money payment, for which you must serve me till the ultimate
sacrifice. And for this I shall be to you according to my testamentary
decree a father and provider, and there will be from me no lie: there

will be much favour, for which I have given my commandment before God. And whosoever is unfaithful and opposed to me, there will be no favour to such from me: his head will be cut off and his pasture seized. For which here is my decree with confirmation and I have signed.

The first day of October, Saturday, in the year 1773.

Making copies from which, you have to send them from town to town, from fortress to fortress.

The great sovereign, the Russian Tsar, the emperor Peter the Third has affixed his hand.

You have to publish the enclosed edict of the great emperor Peter Fedorovich to all peoples, to the Bashkir elders and to all inhabitants on the Nogaiskaia Road, and to all who live on the Sibirskaia Road.

Edict of Pugachev to the Soldiers, About 5 October 1773.
Of our autocratic emperor, the great all-Russian sovereign Peter Fedorovich: etc., etc., etc.

With this my personal decree to the regular detachments I order: as you, my true slaves, regular soldiers, privates and with rank, have heretofore served me and my forbears, great sovereigns, all-Russian emperors, truly and constantly, so you will now serve me, our lawful great sovereign Peter Fedorovich to the last drop of blood. And, leaving forced obedience to your disloyal commanders who corrupt you and also deprive you of my great favour, come to me with obedience, and, placing your weapons before my banners, show your loyal faith to me, the great sovereign. For which you will be rewarded and endowed by me with money and grain payment and ranks: and both you and your descendants will have the prime advantages in my state and will be assigned to perform great service with me in person. Whosoever, forgetting his duty to his natural sovereign Peter Fedorovich, dares not carry out this my personal decree, and falls into the hands of my faithful troops by the force of my arms, he will see my lawful wrath on him, and after a cruel execution.

The great all-Russian emperor Peter Fedorovich.

Edict of Pugachev to the Factory People, 17 October 1773.
Of the autocratic all-Russian Emperor Peter Fedorovich: etc., etc., etc.

This is my personal decree to the Avzianopetrovskii factory to Maxim Osipov, to David Fedorov and to the whole commune my personal order:

As your grandfathers and fathers served my forbears, so will you serve me, the great sovereign, truly and constantly, to the [last] drop of blood and you will obey my command. Prepare for me, the great sovereign, two mortars and bring them to me with their bombs with great speed; and for that you will be rewarded with cross and beard, river and land, meadows and waters, and money payment, and grain, and supplies, and lead, and powder, and every freedom. And you will carry out my orders, you will come to me with enthusiasm, then for that you may obtain for yourselves my royal favour. And if you oppose my decree, you will quickly feel my lawful wrath upon you and you will not avoid the authority of our most high Creator. Nobody can keep you secure from our hand.

1773 October 17.

The great sovereign Peter the Third

of all the Russians.

Edict of Pugachev, 1 December 1773.
Of his imperial highness the autocrat of all the Russians Peter Fedorovich, etc., etc., etc.

I want to keep in my God-given favour each man of those who now want to be subject and obedient to me by their own choice, all my true slaves. And if somebody in his misunderstanding remains aloof from my bounty given to all the people, then he will in the end receive from me great torment and will not be able at all to defend himself. Moreover, just as those who formerly gave their unswerving services to my grandfather the Emperor Peter the First, received no small rewards and praises for being in unfailing service till death for His Imperial Highness, so now I want with all my heart to hear about those who will give me their unswerving services, and after they have served, I will leave nobody without reward for their services. And whosoever recognises this my proven generosity, I have already endowed you all with this reward: land, fishing rights, woods, hives, beaver hunting rights and other advantages, also freedom. Moreover, I promise with the authority given to me as if from God, that you will henceforth suffer no oppressions.

And whosoever does not give any regard to my bounteous charity, such as: landlords, these breakers of the law and general peace, evildoers and opponents of my imperial will, deprive of all life, that is punish them with death, and take their homes and estates as a reward. And since the possessions and riches of those landlords, also their food and drink, have been at the expense of the peasants, thus they have had enjoyment, and your hardship and ruin. And now restored from the lost I have declared for you all, and I have gone over the whole land on my own feet and have been created to give you mercy from the Creator. So, whosoever can now understand and reason out my charity given to you, and every one as my true slave, wants to see me. However, there are still not so many well-wishers for me, as disturbers of the general peace and haters. Now that the Almighty Lord with his inutterably just fate will again raise us to the all-Russian throne, so not one evil occasioned me will remain without retribution: and then everyone will recognise the weight of his crime. And although he will want to resort to lawful obedience and will attempt to promote and produce his unswerving services, nothing will be accepted: then he will sigh from the bottom of his heart and remember his eternal life, but then there will be no return. And whosoever receives this my gracious decree in his hands, he should immediately send it from town to town, from settlement to settlement, and explain the mercy afforded by me to all mankind and remember the eternal life, so that now and henceforth the thing explained above will be useful to all men.

Hereunder is signed thus with His Imperial Highness' own hand:

The Emperor and autocrat of all Russians,
Peter the Third.

Edict of Pugachev to the Peasants, 31 July 1774.
By the grace of God, we Peter the Third, emperor and autocrat of all the Russians: etc., etc., etc.

It is announced for the information of all the people.

With this personal decree we bestow with our monarchical and paternal generosity all those formerly in the peasantry and subject to the landlords, be true slaves to our crown, and we reward you with the old cross and prayer, heads and beards, freedom and liberty, and you may be Cossacks for ever, without demands for recruit levies, poll and other money dues, possession of lands, woods and meadows and fishing rights, and salt lakes without tax and payment and we free all from the evils caused by nobles and bribe-taking town judges of the peasants, and taxes and burdens placed on all the people. And we wish all the salvation of their souls and quiet life in the world, for which we have tasted and suffered from the afore-mentioned villainous nobles exile and considerable poverty. And since now with the authority of God's Right Hand our name flourishes in Russia, therefore we order by this our personal decree: those who were formerly nobles in their estates, these opponents of our authority and disturbers of the empire and destroyers of the peasants catch, execute and hang and treat in the same way as they, not having Christianity, have dealt with you, the peasants. With the eradication of these opponents and villainous nobles, each may feel peace and a quiet life, which will continue for ever.

Given July 31 1774
Peter.

From L.G. Beskrovnyi and B.B. Kafengauz, eds., *Khrestomatiia po istorii SSSR, XVIIIv.*, M., 1963.

c)   **Governmental Manifestos on Pugachev**

Complete Collection of the Laws of the Russian Empire, First Series,
Volume 19, pp. 885-886, No. 14,091,23 December 1773. *Manifesto
on the revolt of the Cossack Pugachev and on the measures taken for
the elimination of this miscreant.*
Through this We make an announcement to all Our true subjects. To
Our extreme vexation and outrage We have been informed that not long
ago by the River Irgiz in Orenburg Province, a Cossack who had run
away from the Don and wandered around Poland, collected together a
band of vagrants similar to himself, and is carrying on terrible brigandage
in the region, inhumanly taking the property of the local inhabitants
along with their lives; and so that he might henceforth increase his evil
band not only with all the miscreants that he meets but also with those
unfortunate people whom he hopes to find still oppressed by the
darkness of extreme ignorance, this miscreant has had the impertinence
to take on himself the name of the late Emperor Peter III. It would be
superfluous here to expose and prove the absurdity and folly of such
a deceit, which cannot seem credible in the slightest to anybody with
only a general human understanding. Thanks be to God! Russia has
already seen the end of that terrible time of ignorance in which by this
same infamous and hateful deceit such betrayers of the Fatherland as
were Grishka Otrep'ev and his followers could set brother on brother
with sword in hand. Already all true sons of the Fatherland have come
to know and then tasted for a long time the fruits of internal peace
to such a degree that even a single recollection of those lamentable
times makes everybody shudder. In a word, there is not and cannot
now be one of those who deservedly bears the name of Russian who
would not be repelled by that insane deception, with which the brigand
Pugachev dreams of finding and seducing the ignorant, who debase
mankind with their extreme simplicity, by promising to lead them
completely out of their subordination to the authorities. It would
be as if the Creator of every creature had not Himself founded human
society in such a way that it could not exist without intermediate
authorities between the Sovereign and the people.
    But the impudence of this miscreant is having harmful consequences
for that region, so that even a rumour of the most ferocious barbarities
being brought about by him there might frighten the people who are
accustomed to imagine the misfortunes of others some way off as the
approach of danger for themselves. And so, indefatigably concerned
for the peace of mind of Our loyal subjects, We hereby most graciously
announce that We have immediately taken the measures sufficient for
the complete annihilation of this miscreant, and with a quantity of

troops sufficient for the eradication of that band of brigands, who have already dared to attack small military detachments previously in that area, and killed in a barbaric fashion those Officers who have fallen into their hands, we have sent there Our General-in-Chief, Major of the Life Guard and Cavalier Alexander Bibikov. Not doubting the success of these measures taken by Us in the revival of peace and the dispersal of those ferocious miscreants in part of Orenburg Province, We remain convinced that all Our obedient and faithful subjects, disdaining the most impudent deceit of that brigand Pugachev as not having the shadow of probability, will never allow themselves to be caught by any tricks of those wickedly artful people who seek to exploit the simple minded and who cannot satisfy their greed in any other way than by the devastation and spilling of innocent blood. However We confidently hope that all true sons of the Fatherland will do their duty and promote the preservation of peace and good order by guarding themselves against those with evil intentions and through the proper obedience to the authorities. And so Our obedient subjects will prosper because of their own state of happiness, to which We will add Our concern, and in which We place and will always place Our whole glory.

Complete Collection of the Laws of the Russian Empire, First Series, Volume 19, pp.1064-1067, No. 14,230, 19 December 1774. *Manifesto on the crimes of the Cossack Pugachev.*

We make this announcement to all the people. It is known to the whole society and has been demonstrated everywhere in much of Our conduct of affairs that, having taken from the providence of God the Autocratic power of the all-Russian Empire, We laid down as the most important rule for Our reign concern for the welfare of those loyal subjects entrusted to Us by the Most High, according to the resolve and to the satisfaction of the giver of every blessing – the Creator, in spite of all obstacles. We have dedicated Our life to giving all people of every degree living in Our Empire a peaceful life without any revolt. And so We apply our constant labour to the confirmation of Christian piety, to the correction of the civil laws, to the education of youth, to the suppression of injustice and vice, to the eradication of oppression, extortion and bribery, to the reduction of idleness and negligence of duty. Our untiring fervour for the general welfare has been most marked in the most recent years, when defending the Empire with a bold spirit from the attack of a strong enemy by Our various under-takings. Not only has he not been allowed up to the Russian boundaries, because of the blessing of God, the justice of Our arms and the bravery of Our victorious troops, but pushed far away from his aggressive intentions. Finally with great difficulty but without mediators We managed to conclude the worthy peace with the Ottoman Porte that we had desired, guaranteeing the external security of the Empire and affording Our loyal subjects the time to take pleasure with thankful hearts in praising God for peace and quiet at such a time. And seeing Us striving with such actions solely to bring the Empire to such a high degree of wellbeing, who will not justly loathe those internal enemies of the peace of the fatherland, who having given up every kind of obedience and daring firstly to raise up arms against lawful authority and go over to the known insurgent and pretender, the Don Cossack of the Zimoveiskaia Stanitsa Emel'ka Pugachev, and later together with him for a whole year carried out the most cruel barbarities in the Provinces of Orenburg, Kazan, Nizhnii Novgorod and Astrakhan, destroying with fire God's churches, towns and settlements, stealing the property of the Holy Places and elsewhere, and putting to the sword with murder and with various torments devised by them God's servants and people of higher and lower degree of both sexes, even innocent infants.

This is an affair of such a kind that it cannot be viewed without horror! It proves that a man weighed down by ignorance, forgetting his duty and the oath given before God to the authority of the Supreme Monarch, and not fearing either eternal or temporary punishment, ceases his obedience to the laws and thus breaks the confines of his obligations to mankind. Generally the crimes of the chief miscreant and his accomplices are many and varied, as was revealed at the investigation, and from the voluntary confession of some of them there was the extraordinary revelation that, committing crimes of various kinds, they themselves could not remember the number of these evil deeds. A description of the unhappy progress of the Pugachev Revolt will be given on a separate sheet.

The investigation of the evil deeds involved in this revolt has been carried out from the beginning at Our order by General-in-Chief Prince Michael Volkonskii and Major-General Paul Potemkin in the capital town of Moscow. And now that it is finished We are sending the verdict and final sentence concerning all the crimes committed by them against the Empire and aiming to make secure the person and property of mankind to Our Senate, ordering it together with the members of the Synod in Moscow and the summoned first three classes of Persons with the Presidents of all the Colleges to hear them from the aforementioned members of the Secret Commission who have conducted the investigation and to carry them out as the State laws ordain.

Concerning the insult to our Majesty, We scorn it and consign it to perpetual oblivion: because these are the only faults in which Our kindness and humanity may have their usual place. We most fervently pray and ask God to turn the sword of His wrath from the Empire entrusted to Us by His wise bounty, and to restore everywhere a peaceful life without any revolt, and to strengthen all Our true subjects living in it and Us Ourselves in all the Christian virtues pleasing to Him the Creator . . .

[There follows the description of the progress of the Pugachev Revolt promised at the end of the second paragraph.]

d)   **Pugachev's Testimony at the Interrogation in Iaik Town**
16 September 1774.

And so I set off towards Kazan, collecting more people from all places.

And before I arrived at Kazan, a detachment met me, which I smashed, and took all the people to myself. And the next day — another small number, which I also smashed without difficulty, and took the people, cannons and all the provisions to myself.

And coming up to Kazan, another detachment was seen on guard with one cannon. I destroyed it and took the bronze cannon, and gathered together some people, others ran away.

Coming up to Kazan, I stayed in camp, and wrote a decree to the Kazan governor that he should give himself up without a fight. And as there was no answer, I ordered forty loads of hay to be brought and made an attack. And although there was much opposition from many sides, I took Kazan. Going into it, I took all that was useful, and quite a few people were killed here. I freed the prisoners from the jail, where I found my wife Sof'ia, whom seeing, I said: "Hallo! [This is the] wife of my friend Pugachev who I lived with in poverty and he suffered for me" saying besides: "I shall not leave you, poor thing." And so I ordered her with the children to be taken with me, and I took them with me in a carriage to the last battle, which was near Chernyi Iar.

There were with me about ten more women, however they were not wives, but only dressed me and prepared food for me, and did all kinds of service.

Here several people of rank were flogged to death with whips. And this interrogation was carried out by Ovchinnikov and Davilin; Perfil'ev was at this time with the cannon. Later the Bashkirs burnt Kazan, and I left Kazan for camp. And as there was no forage here, I went to another place, where I heard the Mikhel'son was coming. And so I armed myself against him. And as my people were not in good order, I was forced to go back to my camp having lost six cannons and several people running away. And I stayed here forty-eight hours.

Later having put my people in good order, I went up to Mikhel'son near Kazan itself, to Arskoe Pole. And there was a battle with him. However Mikhel'son won and took all my artillery and all the baggage seized in Kazan and in other places.

And so I ran from the battle till night. And at night the Bashkirs — however many of them there were — all went from me to the Urals; there remained only the elder Kindzha.

The next day I ran away to the Volga, which we crossed. At this time I had five hundred people.

Having crossed the Volga, I set fire to a village because they gave no assistance, and I went along the Volga to the River Sura.

And before I reached it, there is a certain town, to which I sent the Cossack Chumakov to get horses, he took four officers there and without my authority hanged them. About them the inhabitants of that town coming up to me, said: "They did not resist, so why did they hang our lords?" To this I said: "Although the order was not given, there's no turning back now, let it be."

I came to Sura and stopped. The next day we went along the river, and went up to Saratov. And along the road in towns and settlements everywhere they met me with honour and some we executed through suspicion.

Coming to Saratov, I was joined by sixty Don men, and sixty Volga Cossacks; the commander of the Don men was a bear-mouth cornet and of the Volga men an oak cornet. Coming up to Saratov, I did not send a decree there, because they fired from cannons. And I supplied the hetman Ovchinnikov with a detachment and took Saratov against opposition. Going in, taking cannons and howitzer, I went to camp and, staying twenty-four hours, went off to Kamyshin.

And before I got there several Tsaritsyn Cossacks came up to me. In Kamyshin there was no great opposition. The commander hid in the kremlin, but was taken by Ovchinnikov, and he and others were killed.

From there I went to the Antipovskaia settlement. And the Cossacks from that village went with me enthusiastically, also the Karavaiskie, and others, I do not remember from where.

And before I reached Dubovka a light detachment with Don Cossacks and Kalmyks met me. I smashed it. The officers of the light detachment about whom Ovchinnikov reported were overtaken and given a thrashing. And here ten cannons were taken, and I took as many people as there were, and went to Dubovka where I spent the night.

From there I went off towards Tsaritsyn. Before we reached it, three thousand Kalmyks came over into my subjects. Later Don Cossacks met with me and gave battle, and the Don Colonel was beaten.

When I came to Tsaritsyn itself, the Don Cossacks did not dare to give battle, although they were at the town. Later firing began from Tsaritsyn, and it was answered by me. But I turned round to the right side of Tsaritsyn to the place where the Cossacks stood and won them all over to me. The colonels of those Cossacks all went over to the town. There were six regiments of them.

And so I went past Tsaritsyn.

And at the first night camp the Don Cossacks went away man by man; I had not ordered them to be properly watched.

Coming away sixty versts from Tsaritsyn, a certain commander with a great force fell on me from behind, I do not know how. And at dawn there was a battle, at which I was beaten, lost almost all my people, cannons, two young daughters and all the baggage seized by me in many places.

I ran away with the Iaik Cossacks and some peasants, my wife and eldest son to the Volga. Hurriedly, I crossed to an island with my wife in a boat. And as it was necessary to cross further, Perfil'ev remained, I do not know why, and with him several people of my host.

Crossing from the Volga island to the flood-plain side and going off several versts, we stopped for the night.

From there I sent a colonel of my troop, Pustobaev, with one Cossack to seek the clothing lost by him, which he wanted to find, and Perfil'ev, but having set off he did not return.

I went off to the steppe with the Cossacks, of whom there were sixty-four people. Later we discussed: where shall we go? And after many discussions we agreed to go to the Uzen, and there, collecting more people, to go to the lower reaches of the Iaik, collect Cossacks there, take Gur'ev, board boats on the sea and sail to whatever hordes there were, to come to an agreement with them and return to Russia.

When we arrived at the Uzen, then the high-ranking people of my troop, agreeing with others arrested me. And as this was done beyond the River Uzen and carried out by not many people, because the larger part of my troop, the Cossacks, remained on the other side of the river, so I hoped to gallop off to them on a horse, and persuade them to stand up for me and tie up those who had arrested me. However when I galloped off, Ivan Tvorogov with others overtook me and caught me and led me a whole day and night on a bad horse.

And as they started to eat at a certain time, I seized a sabre and wanted to cut down those people who had arrested me first, that is, the instigators Fedulev and Chumakov. However I was overpowered and an even closer watch was kept on me.

And so they took me to Iaik Town.

Later there came to our troop a Cossack Lieutenant sent from the town to whom, talking with my former adherents, I said finally: "Why if you have thought of taking me into the town have you not bound me?" And so my adherents thought still at that time that I was sovereign and they did not want to bind me. Later the aforesaid Lieutenant put me in chains.

And so I was brought into Iaik Town to the secret commission, where I was interrogated about everything written above.

In conclusion I say this.

When I was still going to Kazan the Iaik Cossacks asked me to go to Moscow and further to which I agreed. When I was defeated near Kazan and crossed the Volga with a small number of people, although I collected a great troop, I had already decided not to go to Moscow, and to pick my way down, whithersoever it was agreed. Before we reached

Saratov, the Cossacks talked me round to going with my whole troop, when it was large enough, to Iaik Town to spend the winter there and go again to Rus to complete my intention. The nobles and officers I killed mostly at the persuasion of the Iaik Cossacks, and I was myself by no means so cruel, but did not spare those who oppressed their peasants or the commanders — their subordinates; also I executed them without investigation, if any peasant reported landlords for tax exactions. I did not have soldiers for this in my troop because they were not suitable for my service. And when there was a necessity for infantry then I ordered the Cossacks to dismount to do everything like soldiers.

A further intention, to possess the whole Russian kingdom, I did not have because, considering myself, I did not think I was capable of government, because of my illiteracy. And I went because if I succeeded in somehow advancing myself or was killed in war, — surely I deserved death, it was better to die in war.

Savra Mavrin carried on the interrogation in Iaik Town in a special secret commission.

From R.V. Ovchinnikov, ed., "Sledstvie i sud nad E.I. Pugacheva," *Voprosy istorii*, 4, 1966.

e)   **A Contemporary Noble writes about Pugachev**

1

I had only just managed to send my horses home, when my hearing was struck by a general rumour which suddenly spread through the people of all Moscow and which shook me to the core and made me regret a thousand times that I had sent my horses away. People immediately began to speak and everybody began to speak openly about the great and incredible successes of the miscreant Pugachev. Particularly that he with his evil band had not only smashed all the military detachments sent out to suppress him, but had collected together almost an army of thoughtless and blind adherents and not only sacked and destroyed everything and hanged in evil executions all the nobles and lords, but also taken, sacked and destroyed Kazan itself and was already seeming to make directly for Moscow, and this was confirmed as a danger posed every minute by his accomplices.

Now judge for yourself how it was with me then when I suddenly heard all this at a time when thoughts about Pugachev had not gone out of the heads of all our people, and we were all convinced, that all the lower orders and the mob, and particularly all the slaves and our servants, were secretly in their hearts, when not openly, given over to this miscreant, and all generally revolted in their hearts, and were ready at the least spark to make fire and flame. The example of the recent terrible rebellion in Moscow was still fresh in our memories, and we not only feared something similar, but expected it every minute. The stupidity and extreme foolhardiness of our lower classes were too familiar, and in such conditions we could not rely even on the loyalty of our own servants, and not without foundation considered them rather our prime and most wicked enemies, and particularly after hearing how they were treating their masters in the remote and, at that time, unfortunate places, and how they either stifled them themselves or handed them over to the miscreant Pugachev for execution, we watched and waited for the flame of revolt and of popular rebellion to burst out as soon as he got anywhere near Moscow. And as we did not doubt that in such a case the first attempt of the rabble would be on the house of Prince Volkonskii, who was then the Commander-in-Chief of Moscow, and this house was quite near to our apartment, and for security the whole square before it was set with cannon, – all this made us indescribably alarmed and terrified, and gave me cause to regret that I had hurried to send my horses to the country and remained in Moscow with only one man and him not very reliable, and had thus deprived myself of the means and possibility of leaving everything and galloping off to the country at the first sign of the beginning of the rebellion. In a word, we all considered ourselves lost in this circumstance and did not know what to do and what to think.

2

I cannot now in any way forget an annoying incident which took place during their departure. As all these people, issued with everything necessary, were presented to me for inspection, it seemed to me a good thing to address them and to exhort them that, in case the affair should come to a battle, they should remember whose they were and not shame themselves before the whole world with cowardice, and should fight well, and turning to one of them, the strongest and smartest of the lot I said: "They won't want to fight with him, one of him could clean up ten of them." "Yes," he said to me smiling wickedly, "if I started to fight with my brother! And if it be you, the boyars, I shall be ready to fix ten on this spear." Hearing this, I stiffened, and swallowing this bitter pill, could only say: "Idiot! Son of a bitch! How this demeans you!" I thought to myself: "That's how these protectors and defenders are in their hearts, and there you are expecting good from them." Later, having asked for his name and written it in a notebook to remember it, I said to him further: "All right, all right, brother! Be off with you! Perhaps things won't turn out for you in this way, and then we'll see." My muzhik lost his nerve when he heard and saw that his name was written down; but since nothing could be done about it and he babbled on so stupidly and carelessly, he went off with the others hanging his head. Later he was rapped on the knuckles for this in a clever fashion; because when he happened to commit an offence and it was necessary to punish him, I remembered these words and trebled his punishment for them.

3

At this time Moscow was completely concerned with Pugachev alone. This monster had already been brought to it, was kept chained up, and all Moscow was talking about him, gathered together to see this miscreant as some kind of freak. At the order of the Empress, he was undergoing a formal and most important state trial like any state criminal and nobody doubted that he would be executed . . . .

Already we found the whole of Bolotovo Square and all the roads leading to it from the Kamennyi Most filled with a throng of people. I as a stranger was so happy that I had with me a companion who knew all the police and who soon found out everything there. Grabbing hold of me, he did not so much run as fly, and poked his nose in everywhere to find out the best place for a view. Soon after this we saw a young man being taken along in a high cart accompanied by a great convoy of mounted troops. He sat next to somebody, and opposite him sat a priest. The vehicle was built in some special fashion and was completely open, so that all the people might see the miscreant. Everybody looked at him with great interest and a small buzz and whisper ran round the crowd because of this. But we had no time to look for long on this slow-moving procession, and rushed to the scaffold after a few minutes to get the best viewing position for ourselves. All this was surrounded for a certain considerable distance by a tight front of soldiers placed there with loaded firearms, and none of the common people were allowed inside this wide circle. But they let through my companion as somebody they knew and me as well, besides which we were nobles, and they let through nobles and lords without hindrance. And since there were a great number of them here because Pugachev had risen up mainly against them, this event and spectacle could be considered and called a true *triumph* of the nobles over their common enemy, this miscreant.

With Mr. Obukhov we succeeded in breaking through the crowd of lords right up to the scaffold and stood no more than about twenty feet from it, and on the eastern side of it where Pugachev was to stand to hear the whole judgement and sentence of the senate being read to him. And so, we had the most advantageous and best place for viewing, and while they were bringing him along, we had time to take a look at the scaffold and everything around it, quite a large space inside the circle. The scaffold had been put in the middle of it, it was four-sided and about ten feet wide, covered on all sides with boards, and with quite a big platform on top surrounded by a balustrade. The only access to this was a ladder on the southern side. In the middle of the platform a pillar had been erected and a wheel lifted up on it and at the top of it there was a sharp iron point. Around the scaffold for about a hundred and twenty feet there was a circle of several gibbets on all sides, not more than ten feet in height or perhaps lower, with nooses hanging on them and short ladders placed against them. By the side of each of them we could see that hangmen were ready and the prisoners due to be executed were held by guards. And likewise there were some other members of the evil band in chains at the foot of the scaffold itself.

The cart with the miscreant had not reached the scaffold when they dragged him from it and took him up the ladder, placing him on the edge of its eastern side opposite us. In an instant the whole platform became full of hangmen, prisoners and policemen, because his closest associates and friends were to finish their lives together with him on the scaffold, for which reason there were blocks and axes on all corners and sides of it. By the side of Emel'ka Pugachev himself there suddenly appeared a secretary with the senate's decision in his hands, and before him below near us, mounted on a horse, the then chief of police, Mr. Arkharov . . . .

He (Pugachev) stood in a long raw sheepskin coat, almost struck dumb and beside himself, and he had just crossed himself and prayed. His appearance and manner seemed to me not at all to correspond to the acts for which this monster was responsible. He did not resemble so much a bestial and cruel brigand as some small victualler or shabby cook. His beard was small and his hair dishevelled and his whole appearance completely insignificant and so little like the late Emperor Peter the Third, whom I had happened to see as close up many times . . . .

As soon as the announcement was finished, they took off the condemned man's coat and all his clothes and started to put him on the block for chopping up as had been decreed, first his arms and legs, then his head. There were many people who thought that a gracious pardon might be given — parasites wanted this, and all good men feared it. But this fear was unfounded: his crime was to big for him to deserve any mercy. Moreover the Empress herself did not want to interfere in this business, and handed it over completely to the discretion of the senate; and so he had to receive irrevocably the reward for all his evil-doing. Then something completely unexpected and strange took place during his execution, for instead of cutting off his arms and legs before quartering him as decreed, the executioner suddenly cut off his head first, and God alone knows how this was done: neither had the executioner been bribed to make him suffer less nor had it occurred because of the error and confusion of an executioner who had never before in his life carried out capital punishment; but whatever it was, we heard only that some official standing near him suddenly shouted out with emotion: "Ah, son of a bitch! What you did!" and then: "now, quickly — arms and legs". At the same moment, there was a dismemberment on the other blocks, and in an instant the head of Mr. Pugachev found itself stuck on the iron point on top of the pillar, and his cut-off members and bloody body were lying on the wheel. And at the same time all the men due to be hanged were pushed from the ladders so that we were able to look round and see them all hanging down and the ladders taken away. A great buzz of gasps and exclamations then went round the whole countless crowd that was looking on this unusual spectacle.

And so this execution was completed and this strange and bloody infamy brought to an end. Later all the parts of the body of this miscreant had to be transported to the various parts of the town and burnt there at the places appointed, and then the ashes scattered to the winds . . . .

From L.G. Beskrovnyi and B.B. Kafengauz, eds., *Khrestomatiia po istorii SSSR, XVIIIv*, M., 1963.

9. The Institution of the Administration of the Provinces of the Russian Empire, 1775

INTRODUCTION

In spite of important legislation introduced during the years 1763-5, local government remained in an unsatisfactory condition, and several of her advisers put forward to Catherine schemes for its further improvement. Broadly speaking, there were two schools of thought on the subject, one stressing the bureaucratic and the other the class outlook. The instructions to the Legislative Commission followed the second rather than the first school, especially those from the nobility, whose spokesmen also painted the darkest of pictures concerning the current situation regarding the administration of both civil and criminal law. Considering the civil sphere, the Iaroslavl instruction complained that:

"The existing extension of cases and the loss resulting from it, forcing the landlords or their stewards, and often the tillers of the soil themsleves to live in the town during farming time, and also the multiplication of affairs, often unimportant in themselves, cause both the courts and the nobility great inconveniences. Many are forced to leave minor insults caused them alone without any complaint, on account of which the farmer suffers losses; the households of the dvorianstvo become hostile to each other, and, finally, frequently repeated insults afford a reason for arguments and killings."

Delays, obstruction and venality were widely condemned. And looking at the criminal side of the law, the Pskov nobles declared:

"The dvoriane and people of every rank of Pskov county, suffer extreme ravages from brigands, thieves, robbers and other kinds of criminal, which stops very many of the dvorianstvo from living on their estates, for the protection of their lives from wicked torment; because of this, the economy and close supervision and good order of the lands of the peasants, etc., decline and decrease every moment. Those living in the provinces, either through necessity or lack of other place of refuge, are compelled for the defence and protection of themselves and their homes to keep up three or four times the normal number of household servants."[1]

Everywhere public order was believed to be at severe risk. Among their suggestions for the remedy of such appalling circumstances, nobles from many quarters of the Empire gave strong emphasis to the introduction of officials elected by themselves, and to the decentralisation of justice, finance and administration. Catherine took note of these complaints and proposals, and of those from non-noble sources, and was encouraged to take action by the Pugachev Revolt. But her own bureaucratic leanings were by no means abandoned, and the ensuing reform of 1775, like several other aspects of her policy, was a somewhat unhappy mixture of the two schools of thought in operation from the beginning of her reign.

The materials bequeathed by the Legislative Commission were by no means the sole source for the reform. In August 1776 she wrote to Baron Grimm:

"Sir Blackstone who did not send me his commentaries, alone enjoys the honour of being read by Her Majesty for two years: oh, his commentaries and me, we are inseparable; he is an inexhaustible supplier of matter and ideas; I do not make anything from what there is in the book, but it is my yarn which I unwind in my own way."[2]

Indeed, the disciple of Blackstone reworked the teachings of the master as much as she had those of his predecessor Montesquieu. While she adopted such concepts as the court of peers and court of equity, she did not by any means intend to make Russian society follow the model of the English. Such an exemplar was to be found nearer home, in the Baltic provinces, where the German nobility had been electing local government officials for many years. The Empress also made use of previous Russian legislation and projects, as well as of the advice tendered by such individuals as S.E. Desnitskii, now Professor of Law at Moscow University, Prince M.N. Volkonskii, the governor-general of Moscow, and particularly by Jacob Sievers, the governor-general of Novgorod. But, as with the Instructions and other projects, Catherine's own hand predominated, both literally and figuratively. Hundreds of sheets of her handwriting, including notes on Blackstone and drafts of the Institution itself, are still extant, and the final choices and decisions were hers, too.

The new provincial arrangements were not introduced immediately throughout the Empire. Smolensk and Tver, with P.V. Zavadovskii and Sievers as governors, were chosen to inaugurate the process, which had been taken as far as the setting up of fifty provinces by the death of Catherine in 1796, with most of the grandees of the time involved in a gubernatorial or other capacity. Discrepancies cropped up between the population sizes recommended in Chapter I of the Institution and the resulting actuality. The necessary money was sometimes lacking, as were the appropriate buildings — in Vladimir province, for example, the officials would not have had a roof over their heads if it had not been for the generosity of the local bishop who lent them an old seminary. Modifications had to be made because of local circumstances: only half a dozen dvoriane were to be found in Viatka, even fewer in

Perm, and the complements had to be made up by army officers; established practices were to be continued to some extent in the Baltic provinces, the Ukraine and elsewhere. Some old institutions, such as the county and the sheriff, and some innovations, such as the viceregency or grouping of provinces under an individual as powerful as the commander-in-chief of Chapter IV below, did not long survive the 1775 reform.

The new arrangements were too complicated for their complete implementation throughout the Empire, and some of them would have demanded a more advanced social milieu, notably the court of equity. Some tart observations on this intended innovation were made by the memoirist G.S. Vinskii:

"The institution of the court of equity, with the important advantage of deciding a case on the spot, to follow equity rather than law in cases of superstition or wild fanaticism, or cases concerning the feeble-minded or under-age, constituted its most important assignment, and forced all Europe to sing and trumpet Catherine's wisdom. The then famous Mercier wrote: 'The dawn of the prosperity of mankind has arisen in the north. Rulers of the universe, legislators for its peoples'. Hurry to the Semiramis of the North, and bending your knees, realise: She first of all has set up the court of equity." But we Russians for whom particularly the great legislatrix has devised these salutary courts, we quickly realised for ourselves that they were just a puppet play. What gifts and knowledge would an equity judge not need to possess in cases of sorcery alone, which are so frequent among the ignorant rabble, who are as much remarkable for their absurdity as their wildness! There have been instances, according to the investigation of the land courts, of whole villages discovered guilty of sorcery, some as sorcerers, the others as the bewitched, as they themselves have confessed. What skill, what powers of speech would judges need, to bring such unfortunates to their senses and to eradicate from them harmful absurdities, possessing them as if inborn! As far as the trial of lawsuits is concerned, these alone could give some positive advantage to the plaintiff, if the Institution had more precisely given this court jurisdiction in such a case. When one of the litigants, and undoubtedly the innocent, has wanted to give his case to the trial of the court of equity, then the other, invariably the guilty, has refused, and the court has not only not been given the power to make him come before it, but not even the right to ask him to write down or to make public his evil opposition. So the wish of the well-meaning to be judged according to equity is destroyed, and slanderers have continued fearlessly to oppress the powerless. It may emphatically be said that the time of the existence of these courts, hardly ten cases have been dealt with by them in the proper manner. I lived four years in the home of the equity judge of Ufa and saw how his Aleshka, a chubby little fellow, drove away from the house the unfortunate Chuvashes and Mordvinians who had come for the justice of equity; how the judge himself boasted that in the twelve years of his judgeship, not twelve cases had come to court. And according to visits to other provinces, the same has been happening there."[3]

Catherine, who herself went on a tour of inspection of the provinces in 1780, did not share the pessimistic appraisal of Vinskii, even he being not nearly so critical elsewhere in his memoirs, but nor did she join in the chorus of unrestrained praise which some of her adherents raised to the new provincial government. Right from the beginning, she recognised that it would require supplementary and emendatory treatment from later legislation, and was to be busy with further schemes for the reform of both local and central government right up to her death. Her work was unfinished, particularly to her own satisfaction, but it was sufficiently complete for it to remain the basis of local government down to the reform of 1864. A considerable measure of decentralisation was achieved by the new, basically two-tiered system of administration, which was placed on the same level as the colleges and rendered some of them redundant. Division of police, justice and finance, if by no means crystal clearcut, was taken further than before. And, most significantly of all, the participation of elected class representatives was firmly introduced. True, their hands were kept off the purse strings and were simultaneously tied by bureaucratic controls (one of which was not the unwelcome reception of a State Salary). Moreover, the representatives from the nobility were to be much more influential than those from the urban middle class and the peasantry. Yet previous efforts to engage the interests of even the nobility in local elective government had been a failure at the heart of the Empire, if not in its Baltic and Ukrainian peripheries, and now, in her tour of 1780, Catherine could find the new machinery working reasonably smoothly in the provinces of St. Petersburg, Pskov, Polotsk, Mogilev, Smolensk and Novgorod. Ufa, over towards the Urals, would no doubt have given her a different impression, if not quite so negative as that received by Vinskii. But in that far-flung region ten years before, the Pugachev Revolt had been in full flame. The fact that violence on such a scale was not to be repeated anywhere in the Russian Empire before the Revolutions of the twentieth century provided perhaps the most conclusive witness to the relative efficiency of the reform of 1775.

Footnotes

1. P. Dukes, *Catherine the Great*, pp.169-71.
2. M. Raeff, "The Empress", p.18.
3. G.S. Vinskii, *Moe vremia*, SPB., 1914, rep. ORP, 1973, pp.42-3.

The Institution of the Administration of the Provinces of the Russian Empire.
Complete Collection of the Laws of the Russian Empire, First Series, Volume 20, pp.229-304, No. 14, 392, 7 November 1775.

By the Grace of God We, Catherine the Second, Empress and Autocrat of All the Russias etc. etc. etc. announce to all Our loyal subjects.

The tsars and the reigns of blessed centuries past and even our own days have given many examples in proof of this truth, that the spread of the boundaries of the state, the increase of the people in it and the resulting abundance of means for internal and external enrichment have so changed the form of their government that it has often been necessary to supplement the statutes, which has consequently made either inconvenient or inadequate those which prevailed during the foundation and early existence of the state; but without taking our investigation to remote times and other states We borrow and put forward a most convincing proof for the zealous sons of Russia from our own fatherland, just as it was in its former position and is in its present situation; because comparing those times with these and the rise of Russia in them, everybody can see with the help of his common sense and sense of history, how much in the present century remarkable for the Russian fatherland its glory, well-being and strength have increased their brilliance; and considering the various former and present circumstances, changes, situations, decisions, needs or necessities, the state land and sea forces of then and now, trade, industry and frequent settlements in clearings and the steppes beyond the clearings, and when there are now not only many steppes, but settlements stretching far beyond the steppes, the former and present condition of Russia can easily be imagined beyond dispute, and in it the increase and enlightenment of the people are taking place, and are themselves arousing the increase in care both for all ways of doing things in the land and in like measure increasing the concerns of the government.

This century began with a war against the Swedish crown; for some years it was unsuccessful, but with the steadfastness of spirit of the sovereign Emperor Peter the Great and the improved organisation of the land forces and establishment of a sea power, it came to a successful conclusion and enlarged Russia with three principalities.

In the middle of these victories, the Turkish and Persian campaigns, this wise and untiring sovereign, sensing the inadequacies which existed in the internal administration of his state and wanting to see the empire at the best level of glory and good order, promulgated and established many different laws and institutions to the advantage of his subjects, strived for their enlightenment concerning commerce and mercantile seafaring, and going into all the details, did not leave any part of the government without new institutions or instructions. Augmenting the state income, he also increased the ways to prosperity of his subjects; he opened up new branches of commerce, industry, handicrafts and trades, founded commercial towns and sea docks; but his life being cut short early, he left many establishments, institutions and arrangements still at the foundations. The many changes which occurred at his blessed death, the different regulations and ideas and frequent wars, although they did not detract from the majesty of the Empire, brought the arrangements of this great emperor either into desuetude, or removed the thought of continuing what he had begun, or introduced other principles concerning the various concepts of things or the changing circumstances of the natural flow of things.

Therefore from the very day of our ascension to the throne of all the Russias, We have tirelessly striven to become acquainted generally and in detail according to changing circumstances with the parts of our internal state administration which demand correction or the promulgation of new institutions, decrees and enactments.

It is known to the world that in 1766 we arranged the convocation of deputies from the whole Empire, in order to find out the needs and deficiencies of each district according to its situation; and we were awaiting the fruits of the labours of the Legislative Commission corresponding to our concern for the general and individual good, when the declaration from the Turkish side of war against Russia in 1768 and its continuation for six years together with many difficult and dangerous circumstances, distracting people from the possibility of the continuous composition of a whole statute and increasing their burden, took up time and thought with an exercise no less important, the defence of the faith and the fatherland from external and internal enemies.

However, blessing good intentions and eradicating unjust and godless enterprises and having given us a glorious peace after six years of uninterrupted land and sea victories with peace and quiet restored together within the wide limits of the Empire, God has given us the time to occupy ourselves with the work so dear to our heart, to furnish the Empire with the institutions necessary and useful for the increase of order of every kind, and for the smooth flow of justice; and so, concerning ourselves continuously like a mother for her offspring, going again into all the details of the internal administration of the Empire, we found firstly: that because of the great size of some provinces, they are insufficiently furnished with government and with the people necessary for administration, so that in one and the same place where the government of the province is carried on, both the state income and accounts are administered together with good order and police, and also criminal cases and civil courts, and the same inadequacies as in the provinces are to be found in the counties and districts; for in one sheriff's chancellery affairs of all kinds and sorts are heaped together.

Very perceptibly stemming from such disorder, on the one hand the delay, neglect and red-tape are natural consequences of such an inconvenient and unsatisfactory situation, where one affair holds up another, and where also the impossibility of attending to a multitude of different affairs in one sheriff's chancellery might serve sometimes as a long-term pretext both to cover up the irregularity of the official and to be the cause of biassed execution of business. On the other hand from the slow execution of business stem arbitrariness and slander together with multifarious other flaws; because punishment for crimes and misdemeanours is not carried out with as much haste as it should be to restrain and cow the insolent. In other places the vast number of appeals allowed brings no small delay to justice, such as for example: in cases involving commercial, mercantile and urban people, he who is not satisfied with the decision of the petty sessions may again sue in the town magistracy, then appeal to the county magistracy, go on from the county to the provincial magistracy, and then on to the senate.

For the eradication of all these and many other inconveniences which would take much space to enumerate, particularly for the institution of a better order and for the unhindered flow of justice, we have decided to promulgate now an institution for the administration of the provinces and to furnish with them the parts making up the vastness of the Russian Empire, preparing for and facilitating the same by the best and most exact execution of the most useful legislation henceforth enacted.

This our enactment, as everybody may see, separates the courts from the provincial government, prescribes for each office the duties and regulations, gives them the possibility of carrying out what has been prescribed, not only corresponds in its system to the present situation of our empire, but also most importantly in comparison with the former system reliably confirms the general peace and security, and provides with varied advantages the private and personal situation and way of life of the different kinds and generations of people living in the bosom of the state; and consequently by its existence creates a new proof to assure our loyal subjects how full we are with humane concern for the people and burning zeal for the general welfare and good order.

And so we hope that every reasonable person and every earnest son of the fatherland, as many as these new institutions concern, will assiduously strive to conform to our good intention and will duly prove their recognition for the boons generally given to our people by this single institution; we ask and pray God to bless this our decision with many years of successful application, to the happiness of our subjects, the increase of true justice, the correction of morals and the spread of all the Christian virtues: and that He will inculcate in the hearts of those being used in this business enthusiasm for an exact and sincere execution of duty, an aversion from the spending of time in idle luxury and all other vices which corrupt morals, and that laziness will be considered a great dishonour by these people, likewise negligence and lack of diligence in everything that they undertake, so that the greatest shame will be for dereliction of duty and lack of concern for the general welfare entrusted to them, and will force everybody and Us ourselves on the path to Him the Creator beneficent in everything, showing to all Our subjects Our customary monarchical kindness. Given in Moscow, 7 November 1775 in the fourteenth year of our reign.

[There follows a synopsis rather than a translation of the Institution itself.]

Chapter I Recommended establishment of the province. (articles 1-46) For maximum efficiency, a province should have from 300 to 400 thousand souls. In the absence of Her Royal Highness, there is a controller or governor with two advisers. There is a criminal and civil court in each province, each with a president, two advisers and two assessors. Each province has a surveyor, an office of affairs of household management and another of management of state income. In the treasury office, there is the deputy of the controller or deputy governor, the director of the economy or of the management of the household, an adviser, two assessors and one provincial treasurer. In each province there is a higher land court, more than one if the size of the province demands it; it has a first and second president, and ten members. If necessary, the province is divided into counties; the provinces and counties are divided into districts. Each of the districts should have from 20 to 30 thousand souls and its own court, with a district judge, members of his court, and two other members, and with a noble court of wards, presided over by the marshal of the nobility with the judge and members of the court. In each district, there is a lower land court with a land executive or captain, and two or three members, depending on the size of the district. In each district, there is one treasurer, one attested surveyor, one doctor, one apothecary, two assistant apothecaries and two apprentice apothecaries. In each town, where there is no commander, there is a chief of police, and in the capital, a head of police. In towns and suburbs, elders and judges of the courts of petty session stay on the former basis. Councils are in the suburbs only. In the towns, there will still be magistracies, each with a burgomaster and four councillors, and a court of wards presided over by the town head with two members of the town magistracy and the town elder. In the province, there will be one provincial magistracy, or more if the size of the province demands it, with a first and second president and six members. Depending on the circumstances, the governor may institute for smallholders and others from 10 to 30 thousand souls in number a court called the lower peasant justice, with one judge and eight members, of whom two are to sit in the lower land court and two in the court of equity for cases concerning their own areas. There are also one or two courts of higher peasant justice where circumstances demand, with a first and second president and ten members. There is also in each province a board of social welfare, with the governor himself as president and two members from the higher land court, two from the town magistracy and two from the higher peasant justice where it exists. In each province there is a court of equity with one judge, two dvoriane for cases concerning the nobility, two citizens for cases concerning townspeople, and two rural inhabitants for higher and lower peasant justice cases. In the provincial government and courts, there is a procurator, an attorney for state cases and an attorney for criminal cases, all of whom are to be found in the higher land court, the town magistracy and the higher peasant justice. In each district there is one attorney.

Chapter II *On ranks* (articles 47-58)
Ranks to be distributed to those actually serving as follows (if they have not already been awarded higher ranks): governor – fourth class; deputy governor, head of police, presidents of the criminal and civil courts – fifth class; the councillors of the provincial government, of the criminal and civil courts, the director of the management of the household, the councillor of the treasury office, the provincial procurator, the first and second presidents of the higher land court, and the judge of the court of equity – sixth class; the marshal of the nobility, the members and procurator of the higher land court, the provincial attorneys of state and criminal affairs, the first and second presidents of the provincial magistracy and of the higher peasant justice, the noble members of the court of equity – seventh class; the assessors of the offices, the provincial treasurer, the attorneys of state and criminal affairs in the higher land court, the procurators of the provincial magistracy and of the higher peasant justice, the district judge, the chief of police and the provincial surveyor – eighth class; the land executive or captain, the judge of the peasant justice, members of the district court and district treasurer – ninth class; the noble members of the lower land court, the town head, the members of the provincial magistracy, the town members of the court of equity, the state and criminal attorneys of the provincial magistracy and of the higher peasant justice – tenth class; the first and second burgomasters

of the town magistracy of the provincial capital and the district attorney — eleventh class; the first and second burgomasters and councillors of the provincial town magistracy — twelfth class; the burgomasters and councillors of the town magistracy in the suburbs — thirteenth class; the elders of the town, the judges of the court of petty sessions and councillors in the suburbs — fourteenth class; the presidents of the higher and lower peasant justice, the rural members of the lower land court and the court of equity — not to have rank, but not to be punished without trial, and to be considered first among their peers in their villages after service.

Chapter III *The manner of appointment to positions* (articles 59-80) The governor, deputy governor and the head of police are to be appointed by Her Royal Highness. For the presidents of the offices and of the higher land courts, the senate submits two people for each place with a report to Her Royal Highness for her choice. The advisers and assessors for the provincial government and offices, the director of the economy, the provincial treasurer, the first and second presidents of the provincial magistracy and of the higher peasant justice are appointed after the suggestions of the provincial government by the senate. For judge of the provincial court of equity, each provincial court submits a worthy man to the governor for his choice of one of them. The district marshal of the nobility is elected every three years by the ballot of the nobility. The ten members of the higher land court and the two noble members of the court of equity are chosen by the nobles of the relevant districts every three years for the confirmation of the governor. The district judge and the land executive are chosen every three years by the nobility for the governor's confirmation. If there is an insufficient number of nobility, the land executive is appointed by the provincial government from officials according to the suggestions of three worthy people from the higher peasant justice. The members of the district court and the noble members of the lower land court are elected by the dvorianstvo every three years and confirmed by the governor. The district treasurer is appointed every three years at the suggestion of the treasury office by the state treasurer. The provincial and district surveyors are appointed by the senate survey department. The district doctor and apothecary are appointed by contract for a fixed time provided they have suitable references. The doctor and apothecary recommend their assistants and apprentices to the governor. The chief of police is appointed by the senate at the suggestion of the provincial government. The town head, burgomasters and councillors are elected every three years by the ballot of the town society, the elders and judges of the petty sessions by such a ballot every year. The members of the town magistracy and members of the court of equity are chosen by the provincial town from the merchants and petty burghers by ballot every three years and confirmed by the governor. The peasant justice judge is appointed by the provincial government from the officials. The members of the higher peasant justice and the eight members of the lower peasant justice, of which two are to be sent to be members of the lower land court, and two to the court of equity for cases concerning their villages are chosen by the villages themselves in the area of jurisdiction of the higher peasant justice, and they are not forbidden to choose dvoriane or educated people or officials or other ranks or well-behaved villagers, every three years for the governor's confirmation. If any of those chosen dies or drops out for some other reason during the three-year period, then the noble places will be filled by the higher land court, the town places by the provincial magistracy and the village places by the higher peasant justice with the confirmation of the provincial government. The provincial procurator, the procurators of the higher land court, provincial magistracy, and higher peasant justice are appointed by the senate at the suggestion of the procurator-general. The provincial attorneys of criminal and state affairs are appointed by the senate. The attorneys of criminal and of state affairs in the higher land court, the provincial magistracy and higher peasant justice are appointed by the senate at the suggestion of the offices. The district attorneys are appointed by the provincial government. Ballots to take place as in the elections of the deputies of 14 December 1766.

Chapter IV *On the duties of the commander-in-chief in the absence of Her Royal Highness* (articles 81-93)
He must keep a strict and exact check on all departments and officials subject to him, but nobody is to be punished without proper trial. He is not a judge but the guardian of Her Royal Highness' promulgated legislation, an intercessor for the general and state good, the defender of the oppressed and the instigator of routine matters, in a word, he must demonstrate goodwill, love and sympathy for the people. The smooth-running of the province, the efficient execution of the laws and the legal general satisfaction of everybody depend on his care. Good order or police in town and country are subject to him. He must eradicate all kinds of abuses, particularly immoderate and ruinous luxury, curb excesses, irregularities, chicanery, tyranny and cruelty. He must intercede whenever anybody is guilty of bureaucratic delay and force the courts to take decisions without interfering in the process, for he is the master of the province, not the judge. If any injustice occurs in the courts, he may report it to the senate and in extreme cases to Her Royal Highness. Criminal cases, particularly deprivation of life or honour, are most affected here; no action can be taken in such cases

without report to him. He must give warning of every possible shortage of necessaries of life, such as grain and salt and so on. He must watch for scrupulous collection of taxes and proper levy of recruits. In frontier provinces, he must watch for security against neighbours, and whenever necessary take the appropriate military measures. The local military commander, even if senior, must obey him on such occasions, also in cases of popular disobedience, or at times of plague, flood or fire. The military commander is responsible for carrying out military orders from Her Royal Highness, but it is for the commander-in chief to supply the troops with everything they need. The commandants of the provincial fortresses, the garrison and army regiments, and guard details, are under the control of the commander-in-chief. The commander-in-chief in the capital sits in the senate in its general assembly and in those departments where business concerning him is carried on, and he is the intercessor there for the business of his province and has a vote like the others sitting in the senate. For escort, the commander-in-chief has 24 men of light cavalry with one lieutenant; two adjutants are given him, and the dvorianstvo sends him an honorary young noble from each district for him to use as he pleases. In the province, the commander-in-chief receives 500 rubles a month maintenance, or as Her Royal Highness indicates.

Chapter V *On the duties of the provincial government* (articles 94-104) The commander-in-chief is the president of the govenment. With him sits the governor and two advisers. When the commander-in-chief and the governor are outside the province, then the deputy governor takes the place of the governor. The provincial government administers according to the laws in the name of Her Royal Highness. It promulgates the laws, decrees, regulations, orders and commands of Her Royal Highness, and of the senate and other appropriate state offices, and checks that they are duly obeyed. It investigates and fines, and then brings defaulters to court. It sees that the regulations of police or good order and of trade are kept and carried out. It stops all illegal disorders immediately, and exercises unswerving diligence to preserve peace and quiet not only in the towns and villages but also in all the land and water subject to it, including the roads. It expedites all business demanding quick action without dispute, such as signed bills of debt or sale, clear contracts unfulfilled. It handles complaints about such matters, and sends arguable or doubtful cases to the appropriate offices. Confiscation of an estate, or part of it, after a court verdict is the affair of the provincial government, as are appeals against delay in the offices subordinate to it. Appeals against the provincial government may be made to the senate. In case of important or extraordinary affairs, or a new general enactment, the commander-in-chief may summon the criminal and civil courts and the treasury office together with the provincial government for their evaluation. If a general enactment seems unsatisfactory in some way, a unanimous representation about it may be made to the senate. When the Supreme Power gives its confirmation, permanent and silent obedience must follow. The governor acts in the absence of the commander-in-chief, and communicates with internal and external counties. He and the commander-in-chief inform the College of Foreign Affairs about correspondence beyond the frontiers. There are two councillors in the provincial government to help the governor, as well as the provincial procurator and attorneys.

Chapter VI *On the duties of the criminal court* (articles 105-109)
It has one president, two advisers and two assessors. It is a department of the Justice College, and sends there important criminal cases and investigations of crimes by officials. Criminal cases in the province which entail the sentence of death or deprivation of honour are referred to it from the other courts in the province for review and implementation. The attorney of criminal affairs may present his suits to it at the order and with the permission of the governor.

Chapter VII *On the trial of criminal cases* (articles 110-113)
The trial of criminal cases will henceforth be in the following manner. Whoever carries out a criminal offence in the area of jurisdiction of the district court, or the town magistracy or council or the lower peasant justice, will be investigated by them without delay and brought to a due conclusion if it does not concern deprivation of life, honour or commercial capital. Sentences of the district court and the lower peasant justice are carried out by the lower land court, and of the town magistracy or council by the chief of police. If the accusation entails deprivation of life, honour or commercial capital after the case has been tried, the district court transfers it for sentence to the higher land court, the town magistracy or council to the provincial magistracy, and the lower peasant justice to the higher peasant justice. They in their turn send on a report to the criminal court, which then sends it on to the commander-in-chief who, in order to strike terror into the wicked, commands the criminal to be punished in that district or town where the offence was committed.

Chapter VIII *On the duties of the civil court* (articles 114-116)
It has one president, two councillors and two accessors. It is a joint department of the Justice and Estates Colleges. Appeals for review of civil cases are made to it from the higher land court, the town magistracy and the higher justice.

Chapter IX *On the duties of the treasury office* (articles 117-123)
It has the deputy governor, the director of the economy, one councillor, two assessors and one provincial treasurer. When the deputy governor is taking the place of the governor, the director of the economy takes his place. It is a joint department of the State Revenue College and the Census Revision College. It supervises household and economic affairs. It concerns itself with the numbers of people, revision lists, information on income and expenditure, revision of accounts, salt matters, liquor leases and contracts, all kinds of treasury affairs, state and public buildings and their contents. Because of the abolition of the State Revenue College, the treasury office is not to judge anybody, but is to take matters in dispute to the provincial government, or to take its complaints to the courts via the provincial attorney of state affairs. The treasury office is to see that no forbidden taxes are collected, and to watch closely for the full and correct registration of income in the province and each district. It supervises the district treasurers, who must give full report.

Chapter X *On offices in general* (articles 124-133)
The offices are to act according to the laws, and are not to issue decrees except to subordinates. Decisions are to be announced publicly at the door of the office, or more generally through the provincial government. If communications between offices of equal standing are held up, then the provincial government can be asked to intercede to find out the reasons. Each office must avoid encroaching upon the sphere of competence of the others, and must not overrule the decisions of others or of itself. Complaints about the decisions of the offices may be made to the senate as they are now made to the colleges, after a 200 rouble deposit and a sworn statement, with the money going to the board of social welfare if the complaints are rejected. The attorneys do not have to deposit 200 roubles since they are acting on state business. Cases cannot be transferred to the senate if their value is less than 500 roubles. Office decisions in civil cases are to be carried out irrespective of transfer.

Chapter XI *On the duties of the district treasurer* (articles 134-137)
Each district treasurer is to watch over all state collections, but he cannot himself make collections or disbursements. He is the guardian of that money, and must keep proper accounts of income and expenditure.

Chapter XII *On collection from the people and on the income of Her Royal Highness* (articles 138-143)
If collections are monetary, they go to the district treasurer. If they are

of grain or hay, they go to the appropriate stores. The lower land court is to investigate arrears, assisted by the treasury office, which is to keep two lists, one of those who have paid, the other of those who have not. Defaulters are to be given four weeks to pay up, then the land executive will go to find out, or a member of the lower land court, helped by two soldiers, paid daily at double rate at the expense of the defaulters. If no payment is made then after three days, then the defaulters are to be dealt with in the manner prescribed to the treasury office. Complaints about the district treasurer are to be put to the lower land court, and the land executive will look at them and report to the treasury office.

Chapter XIII *On the upkeep of Her Royal Highness' treasury* (articles 144-163)
Stone treasuries are to be set up in the provinces with appropriate security and accountancy arrangements.

Chapter XIV *On the duties of the higher land court* (articles 164-192)
There are one or more per province, each with a first and second president, and ten members, all elected every three years from the dvorianstvo. It has two departments, for criminal cases and civil cases, with the first and second presidents respectively and five members each. If there are no criminal cases then the departments share the civil cases. The district courts, the noble courts of wards and lower land courts are subordinate to it, and appeals about them and their attorneys are sent to it by nobles and by other ranks. Those dissatisfied with decisions of the higher land court deposit 100 roubles and a sworn testimony. If the appropriate office decides against them, the deposit goes to the higher land court. Attorneys, who are on state service, do not deposit the 100 roubles. The transfer of cases to the offices is forbidden if its value is less than 100 roubles. If no decision is taken in three sessions of the appropriate office, then a year of its pay is given either to the petitioner or to the schools. Each higher land court has a procurator, and attorneys for state and criminal affairs. It usually meets three times a year.

Chapter XV *On the district court and its duties* (articles 193-208)
Each district should be of 20– to 30,000 souls. Its court which has one judge and two members deals with both civil and criminal cases. It does not instigate its own proceedings until receipt of complaints from private individuals or from attorneys or from a court or from an office. Arguments about land are settled on the spot in the presence of an attested surveyor. Complaints about it are made to the higher land court, with a deposit of 25 roubles and a sworn testimony. The district court retains the money if the complaint is rejected. The transfer of a

case to the higher land court is forbidden if its value is less than 25 roubles. The court scrutinises and publishes at its doors a list of purchased villages. The higher land court should be informed that this has been done, and the senate informed so that they may be announced in the public registers of both capitals. If there is no objection after two years, then no further objection may be entertained. The district court ordinarily meets three times a year. It should complete in one session the case of anybody arrested. If the complaint is made that such a case has not been completed in three sessions, the court's members should lose their year's pay to the arrested person or his heirs, or to the district schools. Extraordinary sessions should be ordered in case of necessity either by the governor or the higher land court.

Chapter XVI *On the noble courts of wards and the duties of this office* (articles 209-222)
At each higher land court, there is a noble court of wards for noble widows and minors. A district marshal is elected triennially by ballot to preside, and the district judge and members of his court take part. Each noble marshal must inform the wards about relevant cases. The wards do not initiate action themselves, but act on the request of widows or the information of the marshal or close relatives or the guardians of minors, or the testimony of two witnesses and a parish priest, or the order of the provincial government or higher land court, or on the information of another court. The wards choose others fit to be wards for estates and for minors, and arrange the appropriate inventories. The court supervises the activities of the local wards, and expects annual reports from them. Widows are to be given advice and support, including attorneys free of charge. The court of wards reports annually to the higher land court, and those who are dissatisfied with the decisions of the wards may transfer their business to the higher land court. The court of wards meets three times a year, more if necessary. For their detailed management of estates and affairs thereunto appertaining, local wards are to take five per cent of the income of minors.

Chapter XVII *On the duties of the lower land court* (articles 223-234)
The lower land court consists of the land executive and two members (or if the district is large — three members) elected every three years. Its functions are to keep good order in the district, to see that the laws are observed and to carry out the instructions of the government and decisions of the offices and courts. It is subject to the provincial government on matters of good order, and concerning bridges and roads. It is to see that prohibited persons do not carry on trade, to keep a monthly record of prices of grain and victuals, to check on weights and measures, to apprehend runaway serfs and punish those who harbour

them (although such people can choose to be dealt with by the district court, or, if there is none, by the lower peasant justice), to supervise roads, bridges and river crossings. It must carry out investigations on the spot without pay. If a large number of people are involved from one village or several villages, the court must move so that the people are not taken away from their homes and work. Verdicts are to be given on the spot. Appeals can be made within four weeks to the district court or lower justice. The lower land court meets whenever necessary.

Chapter XVIII *On the duties of the land executive or captain* (articles 235-252)
As first president of the lower land court, the land executive must effectively and loyally help preserve law and order, public health (in conjunction with doctors and apothecaries), and cattle plague. In cases of widespread disobedience, he informs the authorities and does what he can to restore obedience. He helps to apprehend and punish thieves and runaways, maintain bridges and roads. He (or one of the members of the lower land court) conducts troops through the district. He arranges quarters when necessary, fodder for the horses, wood for construction and fuel, informing the authorities of any abuses. He does as much as possible to reduce fire hazards and to extinguish fires, to encourage agriculture and husbandry, including the mainten- ance of grain stores. He must have especial care for the poor. Runaways and those without passports from other districts should be sent away, and others made to work on the roads and bridges in return for their necessary daily food.

Chapter XIX *On the chief of police and his duties* (articles 253-276)
In every district town where there is no commander, a chief of police is appointed. If there is a commander, he has the duties listed here. In the capital, the head of police has them. The chief of police is not a judge, but must keep the peace and good order in the town, see that the laws are properly carried out, and execute government instructions and court decisions. He commands the local regular detachments, and uses them in times of danger for the protection of the general good. He supervises the eradication of bootlegging, arresting the guilty for the appropriate judicial action. He supervises weights and measure along with the town magistracy. He deals with plague and epidemics, cattle plague and disobedience as does the land executive. He does not leave the town in time of danger on pain of losing his post and his honour. When dealing with a merchant or a petty burgher, he summonses a special meeting of the town magistracy. He must protect those insulted and assaulted, and deal with thieves and runaways, bridges and roads, and troop movements as does the land executive, the problems of fire

prevention and fires, the poor and needy likewise. He must encourage the inhabitants of the town to lawful application in manufactures and industry, and everybody living in the town to good morals and orderly conduct. He is entrusted with the care of state buildings, reporting to the government offices about their repair and upkeep. The head of police does the same in capital.

Chapter XX *On towns* (articles 277-292)

Elders and petty sessions courts in the towns are to be on their former basis, elected by the petty burghers and merchants by ballot at the beginning of every year. There are to be councils only in suburbs elected triennially by ballot, where less than 500 souls of one burgomaster and two councillors, and where large a number of burgomasters and councillors according to the size of the towns. Town magistracies will remain in existence with two burgomasters and four councillors, of whom one burgomaster and two councillors may be on leave in turn, and all of whom are to be elected triennially by ballot by the merchants and petty burghers. All other aforementioned officials to receive at the end of duly performed service an honorary testimonial according them first place in town society after members of the magistracy. And no official may be re-elected into a position lower than that he occupied formerly. The town magistracy or council does not initiate its own business, but takes on cases at the complaint or suit of private persons or attorneys, after a report from another court or sheriff, or at the order of the provincial government or its offices or the provincial magistracy. Cases concerning other courts or offices must be decided in concert with them. Appeals can be made to the provincial magistracy against a magistracy or council on deposit of 25 roubles and a sworn testimony. The purchase of buildings or land in the town is to be confirmed by the magistracy or council after it has been published without objection for two years. The magistracy or council may be in constant session except for official holidays. But they must complete their business in as expeditious a manner as the district courts, or suffer the same penalties.

Chapter XXI *On the town court of wards and its duties* (articles 293-305)

This court is for the widows and orphans of merchants and petty burghers. Its president is the town head and it also comprises two members of the town magistracy and the town elder. The town head is elected triennially by ballot by a town assembly. The principal duties of the town wards correspond to those of the noble wards. The provincial magistracy receives an annual report from the court of wards, and complaints about it also. The town court of wards meets whenever necessary.

Chapter XXII *On the provincial magistracy and its duties* (articles 306-333)

Depending on the size of the province, there is one provincial magistracy or more. It has a first and second president and six members. The six members are elected triennially by ballot by the merchants and petty burghers of the provincial town. It has two departments, for criminal and civil affairs, with the first and second presidents respectively and three members each. If there are no criminal cases, the two departments share the civil cases. The provincial magistracy is superior to the town magistracies, the town courts of wards and the councils of the province. It takes business from these lower bodies by transfer or an appeal, or concerning the attorneys. Many other duties are similar to those of the higher land court.

Chapter XXIII *Of the court named the lower peasant justice and its duties* (articles 334-349)

The lower peasant justice is to be set up – for every ten to thirty thousand souls in towns or districts where there are smallholders or different kinds of ex-servicemen or state peasants or imperial peasants assigned to certain places or factories, post road peasants, church peasants, court peasants and others – at the discretion of the commander-in-chief according to the size of the province and according to the circumstances of the various provinces. It is to have one judge and eight members, of whom two are to sit in the lower land court and two in the court of equity for cases concerning their villages, and they are to be assigned as in Chapter III above. It dispenses justice on relevant criminal and civil cases on complaint from private persons or officials. Arguments concerning land are to be settled by the lower justice with an attested surveyor on the spot within six weeks. Cases which also concern other courts are to be settled in conjunction with them. Many other duties are similar to those of the district court.

Chapter XXIV *On the court named the higher peasant justice* (articles 350-377)

There is to be one higher peasant justice in every province where there is a lower peasant justice, or more than one if the size of the province demands it. There are to be first and second presidents, and ten members elected every three years by the villages under its authority. It is to have two departments like those of the lower peasant justice. It is to be superior to the lower peasant justice and, if there is no higher land court, to the lower land court. It considers appeals from the lower peasant justice and, where appropriate, from the lower land court.

Many other duties are similar to those of the provincial magistracy and higher land court.

Chapter XXV *On the board of social welfare and its duties* (articles 378-394)

In each province there is to be a board of social welfare. The governor himself presides, and its members include two from the provincial magistracy, two from the higher peasant justice where it exists, and for detailed or local information when necessary any district marshal of the nobility or town head for joint appraisal of cases. It is entrusted with the care and supervision of the institution and permanent foundation of popular schools, orphanages, hospitals, almshouses for the poor and the aged, homes for indigent incurables, madhouses, workhouses and remand homes. Schools and institutions with special privileges or under particular spiritual or secular care are exceptional. 15,000 roubles are to be assigned to each board from the income of the province. The money may be invested in mortgages for the nobility as by the bank of the nobility, but these mortgages must be kept in the province and for no more than one year, with no more than 1,000 or less than 500 roubles to one recipient. The money may also be used for the setting up of apothecaries, with the income going to the aforesaid institutions which will also receive medicaments free of charge. Detailed arrangements for the administration of these institutions are proposed. Such institutions may also be set up by private initiative. The board will be in session once a year.

Chapter XXVI *On the court of equity and its duties* (articles 395-403)

For the security of the individual a court of equity is to be set up consisting of a judge, two dvoriane elected every three years for the cases of the dvorianstvo, two town representatives elected every three years for town cases, and two rural representatives elected by the villages for higher and lower peasant justice cases. They must all be conscientious, know the laws and have some education, and carry out their business with humanity. The court does not initiate business, but takes on cases at the order of the government or by request of an official or private individual. It considers cases involving petty criminals of unfortunate backgrounds, crimes committed by madmen or minors, and cases concerning sorcerers or sorcery which contain stupidity, deceit and ignorance. In civil cases, the court attempts to settle disputes, making use of mediators appointed by plaintiff and defendant. Anybody imprisoned without reason being given for more than three days can appeal to the court, unless suspected of serious crime, and the court can decide to free him. Appeals can be made to the higher court of equity. The court meets at the times fixed for other courts when there is business for it.

Chapter XXVII *On the duties of procurators and attorneys* (articles 404-410)
The provincial procurator and attorneys watch out for the maintenance of good order and justice, ensuring that forbidden taxes are not collected and that harmful bribes are eradicated. The procurator interprets new laws and decrees for the provincial government; looks out for abuses of the laws, institutions or decrees; gives a briefing of no more than half an hour's duration on the most important laws, institutions, laws and decrees at the beginning of court sessions; reports to the provincial government about irregularities or delays in the process of justice and administration; gives advice when judges are unsure about the law or when cases concern the public or state as well as a private interest; co-operates with the attorneys of criminal and state affairs, and with them promotes communication between one government office and another; controls other procurators and the attorneys; reports on non-execution of duty not only to the commander-in-chief but also to the procurator-general, of whom he is the eye; looks after those under arrest and visits prisons at least once a week. The provincial attorneys of criminal and state affairs co-operate with the provincial procurator, and have many functions similar to his. They give conclusions consonant with the preservation of good order established by the law and act as plaintiffs with the approval of the provincial government; have the right to demand information on all cases of interest to them; can while plaintiffs also see that the due processes of law are carried out and that order is kept in court, ensuring that its members observe their duties properly; check that fines are duly paid, with double fines for defaulters; but cannot give advice or act as intercessors for others in cases under their jurisdiction affecting the state interest; and must accept the lawful decisions of the courts without interfering in them. They must pay the costs of unfounded cases, lose their positions and undergo the punishments which they attempted to inflict on those whom they have slandered. The procurators and attorneys of the higher land court, the provincial magistracy and the higher peasant justice have duties similar to those of the provincial procurators and attorneys, the district attorney likewise.

Chapter XXVIII *On the establishment of the offices and officials of Her Royal Highness* (articles 411-412)
Lists are given of those offices and officials which may be found in provincial and district towns.

Chapter XXIX *How the provincial government, offices and higher and lower courts arrange their liaison* (articles 413-431)

Provincial government is on the same level as the colleges, inferior to Her Royal Highness and the senate only. The offices are like departments of the colleges. Orders of precedence and modes of liaison are then given.

10. Charter of the Rights, Freedoms and Privileges of the Noble Russian Dvorianstvo, 1785

INTRODUCTION

At the time of the abolition of the Muscovite system of precedence in 1682, the decree of 12 January 1682 proposed that a new register of the nobility be compiled of five basic categories (as in IV, 16 below):
1) Top princely and other ranks, including boyars.
2) Those whose forebears had been in embassies or other important missions during the reign of Ivan Vasil'evich, that is, Ivan the Terrible.
3) Those whose forebears had been given similar assignments during the reign of the first Romanov, Mikhail Fedorovich.
4) Families of middle Muscovite rank.
5) Families of lower Muscovite rank.
A supplementary decree of 27 March 1682 (see IV, 17 below) invited those not included in existing lists to prove their eligibility for inclusion.

As we have seen in the introduction to the Table of Ranks and Tatishchev's "Dissertation", Peter the Great did not create a nobility that was either completely new or unambiguously defined. He accepted many of the arrangements that had been bequeathed to him. This is indicated in his comment on the Synod report of 19 November 1721 concerning the exemption of episcopal *deti boiarskie*, a Muscovite ecclesiastical rank, from the poll tax (referred to in IV, 18 below): "Let it be so for those who are from the nobility judging by their forebears." And in the Table itself, while the emphasis is on service, some deference is paid to ancient blood, particularly the royal variety. The Table too is not without its anomalies and obscurities, some of which were addressed in the supplementary decree of 31 January 1724 (listed in IV, 21 below), where there was one of several attempts to regulate the entry into the nobility of commoners.

The first comprehensive attempt to clear up the problem of qualifications for nobility was made by the Legislative Commission convened during the reign of Elizabeth; however, the Elizabethan code was never completed, and many loose ends remained to be tied up when Catherine's Legislative Commission gathered together in 1767. (The commission or committee of the dvorianstvo set up in 1763 had been of little further assistance, making no positive recommendation on the important question of qualifications, although giving consideration among other possibilities to one broad division between old families, particularly princes, counts and barons, and new, "according to the example of other European states.")[1] As noted in the introduction to Tatishchev's "Dissertation", even the Heraldmaster's Office was by no means certain in 1767 about the precise rulings that it should give in the area under its jurisdiction. Some of the instructions and some of the deputies had positive suggestions on the subject, and passionate feelings. Certain discussion revolved around the Table of Ranks, and the advisability of the continuance of the system contained therein. Ia. P. Kozel'skii, one of the more liberal speakers on the question of nobility as well on that of serfdom, argued that if the ancestors of the more established Russian dvoriane had first received their honours for their loyalty and virtue in service, they could not scorn and belittle those who were now becoming nobles for similar reasons. Prince M. M. Shcherbatov, spokesman for the conservative nobility, was incensed to have ultimate commoner origin attributed to himself and his fellows, exclaiming:

"How can Russia, gathered together now in the person of its deputies, listen to the imputation of baseness to such families as have given her their services through the unbroken course of many centuries! How can she not recollect the spilt blood of these most worthy men! Be my witness, most precious fatherland, of the services rendered to you by your most precious sons – the dvoriane of the ancient families. You will be my witnesses, those very places where, at the wish of our Monarch, the Mother of the fatherland, we have gathered for our security! Were you not in the power of predatory hands? You holy temples, were you not shamed by heathens? Who gave you the hand of help in your peril, Russia? Your true offspring, the ancient Russian dvorianstvo!"[2]

Shcherbatov, the journal of the Commission's General Assembly noted, delivered his speech and concluded it "with an extreme movement of the spirit, which could be detected in the tone of his voice."

The discussion on the Table of Ranks came to no firm conclusion, although several constructive suggestions were put forward as well as emotional appeals. The spirit of compromise, which was by no means entirely absent from the deliberations of the Legislative Commission, may be said to predominate in the Charter itself, where in sections III and IV, ancient blood is given recognition, although more recent service is given greater emphasis.

Section II bears witness to the manner in which the assemblies of the dvorianstvo had become a firm feature of Russian provincial life by 1785. Arguably from 1766, at the time of the convocation of the Legislative Commission, but more certainly from 1775, at the Institution of the Administration of the Provinces, the nobles had come together periodically to elect their marshals and other officials. Jakob Sievers was among those pressing Catherine to make fuller use of the assemblies of the dvorianstvo, and she took a further significant step forward in a decree of 25 November 1778 which transferred to them and their marshals the conduct of elections for which the governor-general or governor had previously been ultimately responsible. Sievers was soon writing to Catherine with enthusiasm of the new arrangements, declaring that "Liberty et Property son toujours ma devise et ma but, et Fidelity et Loyality les moyens pour y devenir."[3] His command of both French and English may have been suspect, but his message was clear. His use of English terms reflected a belief expressed elsewhere that England was "that country which is without contradiction the most enlightened in Europe at present",[4] and implied the hope that the dvorianstvo would do for the Russian provinces what the gentry had done for the English counties. Landlords would be the ally of the government, and would work to the common benefit the more enthusiastically for having been given a measure of independence. If the hopes of Sievers were not completely realised, there could nevertheless be discerned a considerable move forward in that development of local interests among the dvorianstvo which had begun soon after the death of Peter the Great.

The differences between the Russian and English situations were clearly reflected in section I of the Charter, dealing with "the personal advantages of nobles". If liberty begins to cease to exist when the attempt is undertaken to define it, then its presence in the Charter is less than complete. The emancipation of 1762 was officially confirmed, but with restrictions as severe as those in the decree of 1762 itself, for, said article 20:

"at every time necessary to the Russian Autocracy, when the service of the dvorianstvo is necessary and needful to the common good, then each noble dvorianin is bound at the first summons from the Autocratic Authority to spare neither labour nor life itself for the service of the State."

And article 64 in section II ruled that:

"In the assembly of the nobility there may be a dvorianin who has not served at all, or who having been in service did not reach commissioned rank, (even though commissioned rank was given to him on retirement); but he must not sit with those who have been honoured, nor may he have a vote in the assembly of the nobility, nor be eligible to be chosen for those duties, which are filled by the election of the assembly of the nobility."

Moreover, wide though the rights and privileges confirmed to the nobility were in the economic sphere, they were hedged around by a considerable number of bureaucratic restrictions.

At the same time, we need to recall that the bureaucracy was not part of a dominant impersonal state aloof from society, but rather an organisation of administrative offices in which the commanding figures would be nobles like Jacob Sievers and Count A.R. Vorontsov, who wrote to Catherine in the turbulent early 1790s complaining that the Charter had not been bountiful enough to the nobility, which was "the strongest pillar of monarchy"[5] and a chief focus of attack for such enemies of monarchy as Razin, Pugachev and the French Revolutionaries. For all such criticism, Catherine had given the nobility pride of place in the Charter of 1785, although it was accompanied by another for the Towns and thoughts at least concerning a third for state peasants. Restrictions that were laid on the nobles in 1785 were not an indication of their subservience to an extraneous state but rather a reminder that military-bureaucratic absolutism such as was developing in late eighteenth century Russia comprehended the noble as a link in a chain of command rather than as an independent individual.

Footnotes

1. P. Dukes, *Catherine the Great*, p.152.
2. *Ibid.*, p.150.
3. R.E. Jones, *The Emancipation*, p.268n.
4. *Ibid.*, p.268n.
5. *Ibid.*, p.293.

Charter of the Rights, Freedoms and Privileges of the Noble Russian Dvorianstvo.

Complete Collection of the Laws of the Russian Empire, First Series, Volume 22, pp.344-358, No. 16,187, 21 April 1785.

Through God's beneficent kindness, We Catherine the Second, Empress and Autocrat of All the Russias, of Moscow, of Kiev, of Vladimir, of Novgorod, Chernigov, Riazan, Polotsk, Rostov, Iaroslavl, Berlozersk, Tsarina of Kherson-Tavricheskii, Sovereign of Pskov and Grand Duchess of Smolensk, Princess of Estonia, Livonia, Karelia, Tver, Iugorsk, Perm, Viatka, Bolgariia and others; Sovereign and Grand Duchess of Nizhnii Novgorod, Chernigov, Riazan, Polotsk, Rostov, Iaroslavl, Verlozersk, Udoriia, Obdoriia, Kondiia, Vitebsk, Mstislavl and of all the Northern Territories Lady and Sovereign of the Land of Iveriia, the Kargalian and Georgian Tsars and Land of Kabarda, of the Cherkassian and Mountain princes and others the hereditary Sovereign and Proprietrix.

It is known to all the people that in this title of Our Autocracy are not included the kingdoms, principalities, provinces, towns or the lands of others not subject to us or putative; but rather Our largest possessions with their shortest titles are indicated, because they are many.

The Empire of All the Russias is distinguished in the world by the size of the lands belonging to it, which stretch from the eastern limits of Kamchatka up to and beyond the River Dvina, which falls near Riga into the Varangian Strait, and include within their boundaries 165 degrees of longitude. From the mouth of the Rivers Volga, Kuban and Dnepr flowing into the Caspian, Azov and Black Seas, up to the Arctic Ocean it stretches of 32 degrees of latitude.

Such is the present state of the Russian Empire in this famous century, in which the present year 1785 is elapsing. And in this way in the true glory and majesty of the Empire we taste the fruits and recognise the consequences of the actions of the Russian people subject to us, obedient, brave, undaunted, enterprising and strong, who with faith in God, loyalty to the throne which rules it, labour and love for the fatherland strives in its united strength for the general welfare above all, and in military and civil affairs the subordinates are stimulated by the example of their leaders to deeds which attract praise, honour and glory.

Through the course of 800 years from the time of its foundation Russia has found such commanders and leaders among its sons, and characteristically it was each time and with God's help always will be the Russian nobility which has distinguished itself by the qualities for leadership which shine conspicuously. This is irrefutably shown by those successes which have taken the Russian Empire to the present pinnacle of its greatness, strength and glory.

How could it be otherwise? When the most aristocratic and noble Russian dvorianstvo, entering military or civil service, passes through all the levels of command and gets to know the basis of service at its lowest levels from its youth, becomes accustomed to labour and bears it with determination and patience; and learning obedience, prepares itself thus for higher command? There cannot be a good commander in the world, who has not been accustomed in his time to obedience. The highest levels of the Russian dvorianstvo are achieved by those renowned individuals who distinguish themselves either by service or bravery or loyalty or skill, or those who, patiently obedient, by the strength of their spirit overcome difficulties in service, and at the same time increase by their experience their knowledge and aptitudes in the units appropriate to their calling. From ancient times Russia has become accustomed to see loyalty of service, enthusiasm and labour of every kind, and from the throne of our ancestors they have always been abundantly rewarded, decorated with honours and preferred by distinctions. Authentic proofs of this are to be found in the most ancient generations of the families of our faithful and loyal Russian dvorianstvo, which is ready at any hour to take action for the faith and the fatherland and to bear every burden of the most important service to the Empire and the monarch. Later with its blood and life it obtained service estates from which it had its upkeep, and increasing its services, received the estates from the autocratic power as its hereditary lands.

The property received as a reward for its services has naturally made obligatory recourse to those generations of our dvorianstvo which could render their services from the foundations of Russia to our own days, as have the magnificent number of its worthy ancestors, intelligent men, skilful, brave and tireless, who have fought with unshakable zeal and in many different ways against internal and external enemies of the faith, the monarch and the fatherland. But is the proof of the age of the services of their families and of the rewards for them to be found only in the property obtained? Honorary charters were granted before, after and at the same time as immovable property. They are the most concrete remains of their outstanding exploits, for which praise was given as Our most valuable gift and honour to such loving souls. Really where were honour-loving souls to be found more numerously than among the Russian nobility? And did not shame too confirm their obligations? Because shame and abuse are considered the most burdensome punishment to the noble and honour-loving souls, just as praise and distinction are considered the best reward. Such a way of thinking and the reasoning connected with it demand an increase of commensurate size in services, and with the flow of time and many changes in customs, distinctions and decorations in abundance. Coats-of-arms, diplomas for achievements and patents with ranks, together with decorations, have thus ensued as honorary charters granted as a commemoration for each family. In honour of virtues and services, knightly orders of All the Russias have been instituted, as the inscriptions generally attest. The Order of the Apostle Andrew the First-Called for faith and loyalty. Of the Saintly Martyr Catherine for love of the fatherland. Of the Saintly Lord Prince Alexander Nevskii for labour on behalf of the fatherland. And already in our days the service and bravery of the leading Russian warriors have encouraged us to decorate the victors with the Order established for them of the Great Victory-Bearer George and also to institute the Order of the Holy Apostle Prince Vladimir as a reward for military and civil services which contribute to the general benefit, honour and glory.

To you deservedly decorated by the victory order we address our words! We praise you, descendants worthy of your forebears! These have been the foundations of Russia's majesty: you have brought to completion the strength and glory of the fatherland with six unbroken years of victory in Europe, Asia and Africa: on dry land – in Moldavia, Bessarabia, Wallachia, beyond the Danube, in the Balkan Mountains, in the Crimea and Georgia; on the sea – in Morea, in the Archipelago, at Chesme, Metalina, Lemnos, Negrepont, Patras, Egypt, on the Azov and Black Seas, on the River Dnepr and along the great stream of the Danube.

Without doubt these many victories on the edges of the universe will be astounding to posterity. But the eternal glory of the peace concluded in Bulgaria at the camp of our troops at Kuchuk-Kainardzhi on the tenth day of July 1774 by the commander of our First Army General Field-Marshal Count Peter Aleksandrovich Rumiantsev, named Zadunaiskii [of the region beyond the Danube] by us because of this war, with the Supreme Vizier of Turkey, will supply proof beyond oblivion and doubt of their existence.

This precious peace, justifying and bringing to an end with its enactments a victorious war, has by our wish given great advantages to Russia and opened up the way to the aims desired, strengthening its power and its prosperity.

How much the prosperity of the state is enlarged by the blessing stemming from the war is already proved by the bloodless accretion to our sceptre of Kherson-Tavricheskii and the Kuban, gained on the eighth of April 1783 by the zealous exploits of our General Field-Marshal Prince Gregory Aleksandrovich Potemkin, who answered our commands with judicious enterprise and demonstrated outstanding and unforgettable service to us and the fatherland.

Apart from the advantages to the branches of trade and navigation on the Black Sea and the profit which the land brings as it reveals all its fertility, each Russian will always feel deep comfort in his soul as he imagines this country in the times of Vladimir when that prince was enlightened there were holy baptism and brought back from it to all Russia the saving Christian faith, and as he remembers from ancient times to ours how much this kingdom and people now subjected to Russia tore the fatherland apart with their vigorous attacks and destroyed its peace with their devastation. But now that it is our province, that land has been transformed with the help of God from being a source of harm to one of prosperity.

With the new advantages and growth of Our Empire, when We enjoy complete internal and external security, We apply our greater efforts to the constant attempt to give our loyal subjects in all the necessary parts of the internal state administration positive and permanent enactments for the increase of happiness and good order in the future. Firstly we appropriately resolve to extend our concern to our faithful Russian nobility, having in mind its aforesaid services, zeal, enthusiasm and unshakable loyalty to the autocrats of All the Russias, to Us ourselves and Our throne, given to Us at the darkest times both in war and peace. And following the examples of justice, mercy and kindness of those now at rest who have previously adorned the Russian throne, glorifying our ancestors and being moved by our own maternal love and extraordinary recognition for the Russian dvorianstvo, by our imperial decision and pleasure We order, announce, set up and confirm in commemoration of their families for the benefit of the Russian dvorianstvo in Our service and Empire the following articles for all time and with full force.

[The articles are given in summary rather than in full translation.]

The articles are divided into four groups: I) On the personal advantages of nobles; II) On the assembly of nobles, the establishment of a noble society in the province and the advantages of the noble society; III) The instructions for the composition and continuation of a Book of Nobility in the provinces; IV) Proofs of high birth.

I) *On the personal advantages of nobles* (articles 1-36)
The rank of dvorianin is an hereditary consequence of the qualities and virtue of the commanders of ancient times. It is not only useful to the Empire and throne but also just that nobility should be preserved as an honorary status from ancient times, now and forever for a dvorianin's wife and children in an hereditary manner. A dvorianin can be reduced to the rank of commoner only for the following crimes: the breaking of an oath, treason, brigandage, theft of all kinds, false actions, crimes for

which by law honour is taken away and corporal punishment administered, and in cases where it is proved that he has persuaded or instructed others to commit such crimes. A dvorianka marrying a commoner does not lose her nobility but does not transmit it to her husband and children. Without due process of law, a dvorianin cannot be deprived of his dignity, nor his honour, life or property. A noble can be tried only by his peers. He can be subject to disgrace only after report to the senate and confirmation by her Imperial Majesty. If a dvorianin's crimes remain undiscovered for ten years, they should be subjected to eternal oblivion. Corporal punishment cannot be administered to a noble. Dvoriane serving in the lower ranks of the army should be fined as are commissioned officers. Freedom and liberty are confirmed in an hereditary manner to the dvorianstvo. Nobles in service can continue in it or request retirement in the regular manner. Nobles may enter the service of other allied European powers and depart abroad, but they may not spare either life or labour in state service when summoned by the autocratic power. The noble may give himself the title of his estate, whether service or hereditary. He retains the power over any property first obtained by him to bestow or bequeath it, to give it or lease or loan or to sell it to whom he pleases. He cannot dispose of hereditary property in a manner other than that prescribed by law. In cases of conviction for an important crime, a noble's hereditary property is transferred to his heirs. A noble's property is not to be taken away or destroyed without due process of law. Any just demand of or against a noble must be tried according to due process of law; nobody must make himself a judge. Nobles may buy villages, and sell in a wholesale manner what grows in their villages or is produced there by manufacture. Nobles are allowed to have factories and works in their villages. Nobles may set up markets and fairs in conformity with the law, permission of the local authorities and arrangement with other trading points in the area. Nobles may possess, build or buy houses in the towns, conduct manufactures in them, and subject themselves to town law. Nobles may sell wholesale or send abroad from appointed harbours goods which they have grown or manufactured according to the law. The noble's right of property, given him by the gracious decree of 28 July 1782, is confirmed not only to the surface of the land but also to its bowels and waters, to all the minerals and organisms therein contained and to all the metals made from them. Nobles may use the forests growing on their estates in the free manner prescribed in the gracious decree of 22 September 1782. The lord's house in the villages will be free from billeting. The noble is excused personal taxes.

II) *On the assembly of nobles, the establishment of a noble society in*

the province and the advantages of the noble society (articles 37-71)
Nobles may gather together in the province where they have a residence
and form a society in each province or group of provinces. The
dvorianstvo gathers together at the summons of the governor-general or
governor to carry out elections and to hear the suggestions of the
governor-general or governor, once every three years in wintertime. The
assembly in the province or group of provinces may choose the marshal
of the nobility for that province or group. Every three years the
assembly should present two marshals from those of the district to the
state viceregent or administrator, and the governor-general or governor
will appoint one of them to be marshal of the nobility in the province.
As in articles 64 and 211 of the Institution of the Administration of
the Provinces, the district marshal is elected by the local nobility every
three years by ballot. As in article 65 of the Institution, ten members of
the higher land court and two members of the court of equity will be
elected every three years by the nobility of those districts which
constitute the area of jurisdiction of the higher land court, and will
present themselves from it to the administrator or the governor when
the governor-general is absent; and if there is nothing known against
them, then the state viceregent or in his absence the administrator of
the province or group of provinces confirms the election of the nobility.
Ten members (of the higher land court and the members of the court of
equity, the district court and the lower land court) are elected every
three years by the nobility of those districts which are in the area of
jurisdiction of the higher land court from the nobility living on the spot
or those who are written in the list of that province but are not absent
on service or other duties. According to articles 66 and 67 of the
Institution of the Administration of the Provinces, the district or
circuit judge and the land executive or captain, the members of the
district court and noble members of the lower land court are elected by
the nobility every three years and presented by them to the adminstrator;
and if there is nothing known against them, then the governor confirms
the noble's choice. In the case of suggestions to the nobility from the
governor-general or governor, the assembly of the nobility in the
province takes the suggestions into consideration and produces to them
either negative replies or agreements consonant with both the laws and
the general good. The assembly of the nobility is allowed to make
representations to the governor-general or governor about its social
needs and benefits. Permission is confirmed to the assembly of the
nobility to make representations and complaints through their deputies
to the senate and to Her Imperial Highness on the basis of the laws. The
assembly of nobles is prohibited from making regulations against the
laws, or demands infringing them, under penalty of in the first case a
fine of 20 roubles, and in the second case the eradication of the

unfounded demands, which is entrusted to the care and claim of the provincial attorneys. In the capital town of each province or group of provinces, the noble assembly of the province is allowed to have a building, and an archive, and a printing press, and its own secretary and a treasury of its own voluntary contributions for use as generally agreed. The individual crime of a dvorianin will not be held against the nobility in general. The noble assembly does not make an appearance in court, but is defended by its own attorney. The assembly of the nobility is in no case subject to guard duties. According to article 173 of the Institution of the Administration of the Provinces, appeals against the district courts, noble courts of wards and lower rural courts are all taken to the higher land courts, as are all cases, complaints and suits of one noble against another, both civil and criminal cases, concerning estates, advantages, privileges, testaments concerning hereditary property and the right of heredity, arguments about possession, suits about the disgrace and the law of the attorneys; also all cases of those other ranks which by the laws of appeal to the district and lower courts pertain directly to the higher land court. According to articles 20 and 209 of the Institution, in every district court there will be an office called the court of wards for noble widows and minors, with the local marshal of the nobility in charge and the local judge and his colleagues in co-operation according to articles 21 and 210 and 213. A noble with less than 100 roubles income from his villages or younger than 25 years old cannot be elected for any of the duties listed for election in the Institution. A dvorianin who himself has no village and is younger than 25 years may be present but has no vote. A dvorianin who has not served or who has not attained commissioned rank in service (even though it is given to him on retirement) may attend the assembly but must not sit with those who were so honoured or vote or be elected to office. A noble disgraced by the court or whose obvious and dishonourable conduct is known to all, even though not yet judged, may be excluded from the assembly while it is being proved. We revive the order of blessed memory of our ancestors promulgated at the destruction (in agreement with the request of the nobles themselves) of the Muscovite system of precedence harmful to the state, and command future generations to remember: in each province to compile a Book of the Nobility, in which the dvorianstvo of that province should be inscribed, so that each noble family of dvorianstvo may the more fully continue its achievement and name in an hereditary manner, unbroken and unshaken and unharmed from generation to generation, from father to son, grandson, great grandson and to lawful descendants, while God pleases to continue their succession. One deputy to be elected every three years to keep the Book of Nobility in each district in co-operation with the marshal of the nobility of the province. In the

Book of the Nobility of each province or group of provinces the name and title is to be included of each noble who has immovable property in that province or group and can prove his nobility. Each noble in the Book of the province or group of provinces may attend the assembly of that province or group on the attainment of his majority. To the dvorianstvo of each province or group of provinces we order to be given a charter with our signature and the state seal affixed and the privileges listed above and below copied out word for word.

III) *The instructions for the composition and continuation of the Book of Nobility in each province or group of provinces* (articles 72-90)
The district marshal must write down in the approved alphabetical order all the families owning immovable property in the district, pointing out particularly: who is married and to whom; how many children, of what sex and name; bachelor or widow; how many souls of both sexes, living on which farms and in which villages; whether living in the district or elsewhere; of what rank; in service or retirement. Such a list is to be sent to the provincial marshal of that province or group of provinces, with a copy kept by the district marshal. The provincial marshal is to make the genealogical Book for the province with the assembled district marshals from their lists. The genealogical Book is to be divided into six parts in alphabetical order: 1) families of actual dvorianstvo, i.e. with diploma, coat-of-arms and seal received from Us and other crowned heads, or of actual dvorianstvo up to 100 years; 2) families of military dvorianstvo, i.e. all commissioned officers as in Peter I's decree of 16 January 1721; 3) families of eight-class dvorianstvo, as in point 11 of the Table of Ranks; 4) foreign families, as in the decree of 1686, with all immigrant families in a special part of the Book; 5) families distinguished by their title, i.e. those made prince or count or baron and so on by a crowned head; 6) all ancient noble families of dvorianstvo, who can prove their status for more than 100 years, but whose noble beginnings are hidden in ignorance. No family is to be written in the provincial Book if it cannot undeniably prove its dvorianstvo, either with an original document or an attested copy. A two-thirds vote of the district marshals for or against means a charter with the seal of the assembly of the dvorianstvo of the province for each family, or a written rejection. The provincial assembly is to decide how much each family should put into the treasury of the dvorianstvo, but it should never be more than 200 roubles. Appeal against the written rejection can be made to the Heralds. The genealogical Book of the province or group of provinces is to be read out to the assembly of the dvorianstvo, and if the assembly requests it, the minutes of the meeting of the marshals too. One copy of the Book is to be kept in the archive of the provincial assembly of the dvorianstvo,

and the other is to be sent to the senate for the Heralds. Estates in the province coming into anybody's legal possession are to be added into the genealogical Book as soon as possible, and that person is to be given a charter with seal and admitted to the noble assembly.

IV) *Proofs of high birth* (articles 91-92)

Nobles are either born, or created by monarchs. Proofs are many, various and often complicated, particularly because of the different and ancient origins of our noble families. Undeniable proofs of nobility can be: 1) diplomas from Us, Our predecessors or other crowned heads; 2) coats-of-arms granted by sovereigns; 3) patents to appropriate ranks; 4) proof that a knightly Russian order has decorated the individual; 5) proofs from granted or honorary charters; 6) decrees granting lands or villages; 7) award of estates by noble service; 8) decrees or charters making estates hereditary; 9) decrees or charters to villages or estates, even if they have gone out of the family's possession; 10) decrees or charters given to a dvorianin as ambassador, envoy or other diplomatic emissary; 11) proof of the service in the dvorianstvo of ancestors; 12) proofs that the father and grandfather led lives in the appropriate status or service, attested by 12 nobles; 13) bills of sale, mortgage, inventory or testament; 14) hereditary proofs; 15) decrees in which there is proof of nobility; 16) decrees attached to the genealogical Book compiled at the time of the abolition of the Muscovite system of precedence; 17) the supplementary decree of 27 March 1682; 18) the resolution of Peter I on the Synod report of 19 November 1721 concerning episcopal *deti boiarskie;* 19) point 15 of the Table of Ranks on serving commissioned officers, as well as the explanatory note to the effect that personal or life peers (civil and court ranks below rank 8) are not to be included in the genealogical Book; 20) three generations of personal dvorianstvo, with the third enabled to petition for hereditary dvorianstvo after 20 years honorable service; 21) the decree of 31 January 1724 concerning civil service secretaries and military ensigns; 22) point 16 of the Table of Ranks, concerning foreigners of proven nobility.

In confirmation of all this, We have signed with Our own hand this our granted Charter of the Rights, Freedoms and Advantages of Our truly loyal Russian dvorianstvo, and We have ordered it to be ratified with Our state seal in our capital city of Saint Peter, 21 April 1785, the twenty-third year of our reign.

Select Translations of Terminology

Alternative translations and fuller definitions may be found in S.G. Pushkarev, comp., *Dictionary of Russian Historical Terms from the Eleventh Century to 1917*, New Haven, 1970.

barshchina — labour service, corvée
blagopoluchie — happiness
bobyl — poor landless peasant, labourer
chernososhnye — state peasants (certain category of)
chin — rank, grade
dolzhnost — duty, personal office, function
domostroitel'stvo — household management
dvorianin, dvorianstvo — noble, nobility
dvorovye liudi, krest'iane — people, peasants of the lord's household
glava — head, town head
glavnokomanduiushchii — commander-in-chief
gorodnichii — chief of police
guberniia — province
iasak — tribute
kazennaia palata — state office
korpus — school, academy
meshchanin, meshchanstvo — petty burgher/s, petty bourgeois/ie
mestnichestvo — system of preferment or precedence
namestnik, namestnichestvo — viceregent, viceregency or province/s
nizhnaia rasprava — lower peasant justice
nizhnii zemskii sud — lower land court
ober-politseimeister — head of police
obrok — quitrent
odnodvortsy — small farm holders
opeka — court of wards
palata — office
podushnaia podat — poll-tax
pomest'e — estate (service)
posad — suburb/s
prikashchik — bailiff

provintsiia — county
ratman — councillor (town or suburb)
ratusha — council
raznochintsy — people of various ranks
rod — family, line
slovesnyi sud — court of petty sessions
smiritel'nyi dom — remand home
sovestnyi sud — court of equity
sovetnik — councillor (state official)
starosta — elder
striapchii — attorney
tatary — Tartars
tiaglo — household
uchrezhdenie — institution
ugod'ia — appurtenances
upravitel — steward
verkhniaia rasprava — higher peasant justice
verkhnii zemskii sud — higher land court
voevoda — sheriff
votchina — estate (hereditary)
zemskii ispravnik — land executive, land captain
zvanie — title

General

Bartlett, R., and Clendenning, P.H. *Eighteenth-Century Russia. A Select Bibliography,* Newtonville, 1978.

Druzhinin, N.M. and other eds., *Absoliutizm v Rossii (XVII-XVIIIvv.): Sbornik statei . . . B.B. Kafengauza,* M., 1964.

Dukes, P., *Catherine the Great and the Russian Nobility,* Cambridge, 1967.

Dukes, P., *A History of Russia: Medieval, Modern, Contemporary,* London, 1970.

Florinsky, M.T., *Russia: A History and an Interpretation,* Vol. 1, New York, 1955.

Jones, R.E., *The Emancipation of the Russian Nobility, 1762-1785,* Princeton, 1973.

Kochan, M., *Life in Russia under Catherine the Great,* London and New York, 1969.

Pashkov, A.I. and others, *A History of Russian Economic Thought: Ninth Through Eighteenth Centuries* Trans., Berkeley and Los Angeles, 1964.

Raeff, M., *Catherine the Great: A Profile,* London and New York, 1972.

Raeff, M., *Imperial Russia, 1682-1825: The Coming of Age of Modern Russia,* New York, 1970.

Raeff, M., *Origins of the Russian Intelligentsia: The Eighteenth-Century Nobility,* New York, 1966.

Ransel, D.L., *The Politics of Catherinian Russia, The Panin Party,* New Haven and London, 1975.

Troitskii, S.M., *Russkii absoliutizm i dvorianstvo XVIIIv.: Formirovanie biurokratii,* M., 1974.

1) The Table of Ranks

Evreinov, V.A., *Grazhdanskoe chinoproizvodstvo v Rossii,* SPB., 1888.

Hassell, J., "Implementation of the Russian Table of Ranks during the Eighteenth Century," *Slavic Review,* XXIX, 2,1970.

Troitskii, S.M. "Iz istorii sozdaniia tabeli o rangakh," *Istoriia SSSR,* 1, 1974.

2) Tatishchev, The Voluntary and Agreed Dissertation

Daniels, R.L., *V.N. Tatishchev: Guardian of the Petrine Revolution,*

Philadelphia, 1973.

Korsakov, D.A., "Vasilii Nikitich Tatishchev," in *Iz zhizni russkikh deiatelei XVIII veka,* Kazan, 1891.

Meehan-Waters, B., "The Russian Aristocracy and the Reforms of Peter The Great," *Canadian-American Slavic Studies,* VIII, 2, 1974.

Raeff, M., *Plans for Political Reform in Imperial Russia, 1730-1905,* Englewood Cliffs, 1966.

Raeff, M., "The Enlightenment in Russia and Russian Thought in the Enlightenment," in J.G. Garrard ed., *The Eighteenth Century in Russia,* Oxford, 1973.

Troitskii, S.M., "Istoriografiia 'dvortsovykh perevorotov' v Rossii XVIIIv.," *Voprosy istorii,* 2, 1966.

Troitskii, S.M., "Dvorianskie proekty sozdaniia 'tret'ego china',", in V.T. Pashuto, ed., *Obshchestvo i gosudarstvo feodal'noi Rossii,* Moscow, 1975.

3) The Manifesto on the Freedom of the Nobility

Raeff, M., "The Domestic Policies of Peter III and his Overthrow," *The American Historical Review,* LXXV, 5, 1970.

Rubinshtein, N.L. "Ulozhennaia komissiia 1754-1766gg. i ego proekt novogo ulozheniia, 'O sostoianii poddanykh voobshche,' " *Istoricheskie zapiski,* 38, 1951.

Vernadskii, G.V., "Manifest Petra III o vol'nosti dvorianskoi i zakonodatel'naia komissiia 1754-1766gg.," *Istoricheskoe obozrenie* Vol. 20, 1915.

4) Catherine II's Directions to Prince A.A. Viazemskii

Chechulin, N.D., in Chechulin and others eds., *Istoriia pravitel'stvuiushchogo senata za dvesti let, 1711-1911,* SPB., 1911, rep. ORP, 1973.

Hassell, J.E., "Catherine II and Procurator General Vjazemskij," *Jahrbücher für Geschichte Osteuropas,* 24, 1, 1976.

Petrova, V.A., "Politicheskaia bor'ba vokrug senatskoi reformy 1763 goda," *Vestnik Leningradskogo Universiteta,* 8, 1967.

Veretennikov, V., *K istorii ekaterininskoi general-prokuratury,* Khar'kov, 1914.

Veretennikov, V., *Ocherki istorii general-prokuratury v Rossii do Ekaterininskogo vremeni,* Khar'kov, 1915.

5) S.E. Desnitskii's Proposal

Brown, A.H., "Adam Smith's First Russian Followers," in A.S. Skinner and T. Wilson, eds., *Essays on Adam Smith,* Oxford, 1975.

Brown, A.H., "S.E. Desnitsky, Adam Smith, and the *Nakaz* of Catherine II," *Oxford Slavonic Papers,* New Series, 7, 1974.

Brown, A.H., "The Father of Russian Jurisprudence: The legal thought of S.E. Desnitskii", in W.E. Butler, ed., *Russian Law: Historical and Political Perspectives*, Leyden, 1977.

6) A. Ia., Polenov on the Serf Condition

Bak, I.S., "A. Ia. Polenov (Filosofskie, obshchestvenno-politicheskie i ekonomicheskie vzgliady,)" *Istoricheskie zapiski*, 28, 1949.

Beliavskii, M.T., *Krest'ianskii vopros v Rossii nakanune vosstaniia E.I. Pugacheva*, M., 1965.

Dukes, P., "Catherine II's Enlightened Absolutism and the Problem of Serfdom", in W.E. Butler, ed., *Russian Law: Historical and Political Perspectives*, Leyden, 1977.

Polenov, D., "A. Ia. Polenov, russkii zakonoved XVIII veka," *Russkii arkhiv*, 1865.

7) P. I. Rychkov's Instruction

Confino, M., *Domaines et seigneurs en Russie vers la fin du XVIIIe siècle*, Paris 1963.

Confino, M., *Systèmes agraires et progrès agricole; L'assolement triennal en Russie aux XVIIIe-XIXe siècles*, Paris, 1969.

Pekarskii, P., *Zhizn'i literaturnaia perepiska P. I. Rychkova*, SPB., 1867.

Rubinshtein, N.L., *Sel'skoe khoziaistvo Rossii vo vtoroi polovine XVIIIv.*, M., 1957.

8) The Pugachev Revolt

Alexander, J.T., *Autocratic Politics in a National Crisis: The Imperial Russian Government and Pugachev's Revolt, 1773-1775*, Bloomington and London, 1969.

Alexander, J.T., *Emperor of the Cossacks; Pugachev and the Frontier Jacquerie of 1773-1775*, Lawrence, Kansas, 1973.

Avrich, P., *Russian Rebels, 1600-1800*, New York and London, 1973.

Kurmacheva, M.D., "Ob uchastii krepostnoi intelligentsii v Krest'ianskoi voine, 1773-1775," in L.V. Cherepnin and others, eds., *Krest'ianskie voiny v Rossii XVII-XVIII vekov: Problemy, poiski, resheniia*, M., 1974.

Longworth, P., "Peasant Leadership and the Pugachev Revolt," *Journal of Peasant Studies*, 2,2, 1975.

Longworth, P., "The Last Great Cossack Rising," *Journal of European Studies*, 3, 1970.

Mavrodin, V.V., *Krest'ianskaia voina v Rossii v 1773-1775 godakh: Vosstanie Pugacheva*, 3 vols., L., 1961-1970.

Raeff, M., "Pugachev's Rebellion," in R. Foster and J. Greene, eds., *Preconditions of Revolution in Early Modern Europe*, Baltimore, Maryland, 1970.

9) The Institution of the Administration of the Provinces

Bel'iavskii, M.T., "Trebovaniia dvorian i perestroika organov upravleniia i suda na mestakh v 1775g.," *Nauchnye doklady vysshei shkoly, istoricheskie nauki*, 4, 1960.

Duran, J.A., "The Reform of Financial Administration in Russia during the Reign of Catherine II," *Canadian-American Slavic Studies*, IV, 3, 1970.

Grigor'ev, V.V., *Reforma mestnogo upravleniia pri Ekaterine II: Uchrezhdenie o guberniiakh 7 noiabria 1775g.*, SPB., 1910.

LeDonne, J.P., "The Judicial Reform of 1775 in Central Russia," *Jahrbücher für Geschichte Osteuropas*, 21, 1, 1973.

Raeff, M., "The Empress and the Vinerian Professor: Catherine II's Projects of Government Reforms and Blackstone's Commentaries," *Oxford Slavonic Papers*, New Series, 7, 1974.

10) Charter of the Rights, Freedoms and Privileges

Druzhinin, N.M., "Prosveshchennyi absoliutizm v Rossii," in Druzhinin, *Absoliutizm v Rossii*.

Korf, S.A., *Dvorianstvo i ego soslovnoe upravlenie za stoletie 1762-1861*, SPB., 1906

Romanovich-Slavatinskii, A.V., *Dvorianstvo v Rossii ot nachala XVIII veka do otmeny krepostnogo prava*, Kiev, 1912.